W9-CBS-696

SYLLABUS

WORLD HARVEST SCHOOL OF
CONTINUOUS LEARNING

530 E. IRELAND ROAD
SOUTH BEND, INDIANA 46614
U.S.A.

The
GIFTS
&
MINISTRIES
of the
HOLY SPIRIT

By
LESTER SUMRALL
President

This special teaching syllabus is a college workbook. The space prepared for your personal notes is for the text to grow into your own material.

A video and audiotape is available to assist you.

Copyright All Rights Reserved
Eleventh printing, 1991

GIFTS AND MINISTRIES OR THE HOLY SPIRIT
ISBN No. 0-937580-51-1

Printed by LESEA PUBLISHING CO.
P.O. Box 12
South Bend, Indiana 46624

DEDICATED

This syllabus of special studies on the gifts and ministries of the Holy Spirit is dedicated to the late Howard Carter of London, England.

During World War I, Howard Carter was in prison as a conscientious objector. While there, through prayer and study of the Word of God, the glorious truth regarding the gifts was born into his heart.

I lived with Reverend Carter for a number of years and knew personally how he was persecuted by religious leaders because of these truths. Yet, today, his interpretation of the gifts of the Spirit are accepted and enjoyed by millions of people of all denominations all over the world.

I was highly honored to hear him lecture and answer questions on the gifts and ministries of the Holy Spirit many times in many countries.

The charismatic world owes much of the treasure of this teaching to that dedicated man. God revealed to him the *identity*, *definition* and *operation* of the gifts and ministries of the Holy Spirit.

It is another evidence of how great blessing often comes from suffering.

Lester Sumrall

SYLLABUS

WORLD HARVEST SCHOOL OF CONTINUOUS LEARNING

STUDY: THE GIFTS AND MINISTRIES OF THE HOLY SPIRIT

INDEX

THE NINE GIFTS OF THE HOLY SPIRIT

THERE ARE NINE GIFTS

THERE ARE THREE CATEGORIES

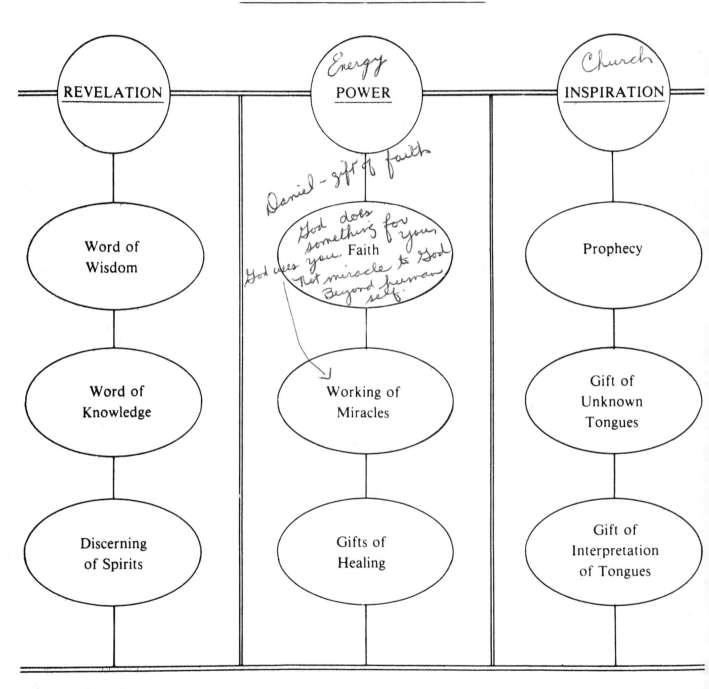

REVELATION

Energy
POWER

Church
INSPIRATION

Word of
Wisdom

Word of
Knowledge

Discerning
of Spirits

Daniel – gift of faith

God does something for you. God uses you. Not miracle to God. Beyond human self.
Faith

Working of
Miracles

Gifts of
Healing

Prophecy

Gift of
Unknown
Tongues

Gift of
Interpretation
of Tongues

Need to follow Bible Method -

#3 Gifts

Power gifts - healings - study healing reports and testimonies
→ Steven Jeffries -.
Howard Carter -
Smith Wigglesworth -
Stay humble before the Lord - no pride -
Give it to Jesus - don't expect something to come back.
Bless them from Jesus. Give as unto the Lord.
Wm. Brannon - error -
Wisdom lives -
God finalizes all healings
39 major catagories of desease
Jesus never fails

Inspiration - Three gifts build up the church Body

① prophecy - spiritual uterance to build up church
tongue for church -
2 or 3 witnesses let every word be established

② tongues -

③ interpretation - edification - edifice → things built up - gives
strength - enlarges - Church built with strength and courage
————→ all three work as one → Chapter 14 I Cor 23

Everything of perfection in universe stamped with 3.
God's devine nature. 3 entities are one in the same -
Teaching syllabus Father, Son, Holy Spirit -

exhortation - encourage - push - shove to keep on Revives
something that is dying
1. strengthen
2. encourage
3 comfort

SYLLABUS

WORLD HARVEST SCHOOL OF CONTINUOUS LEARNING

STUDY: THE GIFTS AND MINISTRIES OF THE HOLY SPIRIT

LESSON 1

INTRODUCTION

Unity

READING:

I Corinthians 12:1-12, *Now concerning spiritual gifts, brethren, I would not have you ignorant.*

v. 2, *Ye know that ye were Gentiles, carried away unto these dumb idols, even as ye were led.*

v. 3, *Wherefore I give you to understand, that no man speaking by the Spirit of God calleth Jesus accursed: and that no man can say that Jesus is the Lord, but by the Holy Ghost.*

v. 4, *Now there are diversities of gifts, but the same Spirit.*

v. 5, *And there are differences of administrations, but the same Lord.*

v. 6, *And there are diversities of operations, but it is the same God which worketh all in all.*

v. 7, *But the manifestations of the Spirit is given to every man to profit withal.*

v. 8, *For to one is given by the Spirit the word of wisdom; to another the word of knowledge by the same Spirit;*

v. 9, *To another faith by the same Spirit; to another the gifts of healing by the same Spirit;*

v. 10, *To another the working of miracles; to another prophecy; to another discerning of spirits; to another divers kinds of tongues; to another the interpretation of tongues:*

v. 11, *But all these worketh that one and the selfsame Spirit, dividing to every man severally as he will.*

Love - tapes audio & video -

① diverse gifts - Same Spirit - Same Lord - same God
   Jesus - Father - Holy Spirit
   ⓐ revelation, ⓑ power ⓒ inspiration

In diversity there is unity. Joined in same spirit
1. gifts 2. service 3. work

all work - self same Spirit (unity) [tatology]
   severally as He determines. vs 11 don't Be too soon
To soon satisfied. -   satisfied
→Blood of Jesus makes you holy.
   (Charisma)

No function } strife, fault finding, bad spirit inside
of gifts

Body many members - works completely together.

12: 12-26 - Love one another. Forgive one another.
God's men have clay feet -
                                          covet with fire
vs. But eagerly desire the greater gifts - (earnest-heat) Best
31   = mighty gifts) gifts)
covet spiritual things - God is inexhaustible

word of knowledge, wisdom, old testament and new 7 gifts -
   prophets of old - Church giant - mighty in anointing -
covet best gifts → yet I show you a better way.
Gifts chapter not love chapter.
Word of wisdom - best - prophetic ministry - old prophets
Ez. 3: 17-19

v. 12, *For as the body is one, and hath many members, and all the members of that one body, being many, are one body: so also is Christ.*

1. BIBLICAL REVELATION

The works of the Holy Spirit are revealed in pristine grandeur.

A. In His creation world: The Holy Spirit is omnipotent. He is all powerful.

Genesis 1:2, *And the earth was without form, and void; and darkness was upon the face of the deep. And the spirit of God moved upon the face of the waters.*

B. In His universality: Psalm 139:7, *Whither shall I go from thy spirit? or whither shall I flee from thy presence?* The Holy Spirit is shown as being omnipresent.

C. In His conviction of sin: Genesis 6:3, *And the LORD said, My spirit shall not always strive with man, for that he also is flesh: yet his days shall be an hundred and twenty years.* Here the Holy Spirit is striving to bring man to a place of reconciliation with God.

D. Prophetically: During this present dispensation of grace God promised to pour out His Spirit upon all flesh. Joel 2:28, *And it shall come to pass afterward, that I will pour out my spirit upon all flesh; and your sons and your daughters shall prophesy, your old men shall dream dreams, your young men shall see visions.*

E. By revelation or prophecy Jesus said in John 16:13, *Howbeit when he, the Spirit of truth, is come, he will guide you into all truth: for he shall not speak of himself; but whatsoever he shall hear, that shall he speak: and he will shew you things to come.*

2. THE HOLY SPIRIT IS THE GUIDE INTO ALL TRUTH.

The Holy Spirit is the revealer of things to come. This is the Dispensation of the Holy Spirit, separate from the Dispensations of Innocence, Conscience, Human Government, Promise and Law.

In these lessons we shall study His gifts and His ministries to the Church.

These lessons are teachings related to the sign gifts of the Spirit.

They are special and supernatural gifts from the Holy Ghost, the third person of the Trinity given to the New Testament Church.

Matthew 16:18, *And I say also unto thee, That thou art Peter, and upon this rock I will build my church; and the gates of hell shall not prevail against it.*

These gifts are the special weapons of warfare against the devil, the world and the flesh.

We must learn of their existence, of their availability to us, of their proper usage, and we must understand their limitations, as well as their potential.

SYLLABUS

WORLD HARVEST SCHOOL OF CONTINUOUS LEARNING

STUDY: THE GIFTS AND MINISTRIES OF THE HOLY SPIRIT

LESSON 2

THE CHARISMA

INTRODUCTION:

The Christian world is excited about charisma. Charismatic meetings are the "in thing" worldwide.

READING:

I Peter 4:10, *As every man hath received the gift. . .minister the same. . .*

II Corinthians 3:6, *. . .our sufficiency is from God, who also made us sufficient as ministers of the new covenant, not of the letter but of the Spirit; for the letter kills, but the Spirit gives life* (NKJ).

1. WHAT IS CHARISMA?

The Greek word for spiritual gift is *charisma*. It means, "something freely given." In its characteristic usage, it denotes an extraordinary ability bestowed by the Holy Spirit for special service. That is the reason I call these gifts "the weapons of our warfare." They are the gifts from the Holy Spirit to enable the church to defeat any enemy which comes against it. The plural Greek word, *Charismata*, is found in I Corinthians 12:4, 9, 28, 30. The spiritual gifts of *charisma* are operations of supernatural *revelation*, *power* and *inspiration*, to secure the church against the devil, the world and the flesh. These gifts show an encounter with God. The gifts represent a co-action with the human personality and divine powers of God working together. It is divine-human interworking.

2. CHARISMA IS PROPHETIC

The only way the fulfillment of Joel 2:28 could possibly happen, is for diversification to take place in the body of Christ, the Church. To retain the move of the Spirit in one denominational group would be to eliminate the largest portion of the church. Therefore, God sent the Holy Spirit into every major denomination on the face of the earth. The work of the Holy Spirit can be seen in Catholics, Episcopalians, Lutherans, Baptists, Methodists, etc. This was the only means to ensure that the blessing would reach the total world population.

3. THE GLOBAL CHARISMA

This charismatic move of God is the hope of the modern church. While one group of Christians are handing out propaganda that God is dead, that miracles are not for today, that speaking in tongues ended with the first century church; an army of Spirit-filled believers from every denominational background marches toward the glorious return of the Lord Jesus Christ. The charismatic move of God is global.

4. THE CHURCH FACES THE CHALLENGE

One of the great dangers facing the modern Church is that it will become one great referral station.

A. It will refer the alcoholic to Alcoholics Anonymous.

B. It will refer the emotionally distraught to the psychiatrists.

C. It will refer domestic problems between husbands and wives to psychologists, consulting clinics and attorneys.

D. It will refer the incorrigible teenager to a house of correction.

E. It will refer the mentally unbalanced to an asylum.

The Holy Spirit move of God teaches that Christ is the answer **right now.**

The key to this truth is the operation of the gifts of the Holy Spirit. They are the weapons of our warfare. (Ephesians 6:10-18; II Corinthians 10:4-5).

SYLLABUS

WORLD HARVEST SCHOOL OF CONTINUOUS LEARNING

STUDY: THE GIFTS AND MINISTRIES OF THE HOLY SPIRIT

LESSON 3

HISTORIC AND GLOBAL COMMUNICATION

INTRODUCTION:

God speaks and communicates to His people. The gifts of the Spirit are the powerful tools and means for this divine communication.

READING:

Zechariah 4:6, . . .*Not by might, nor by power, but by my spirit, saith the LORD of hosts.*

1. **COMMUNICATION**

   A. The gifts of the Spirit are primarily divine communications transmitted from the Holy Trinity through the channel of the Holy Spirit into the church of the Lord Jesus Christ.

   B. The gifts of the Spirit primarily function in three vast areas. They are in the area of *revelation, power* or *energy,* and *inspiration.* These are the three areas in which the church of Jesus Christ is an invincible force, stronger than any power known on the face of this earth.

2. **A CONQUERING CHRIST**

   Jesus Christ came to this earth to redeem and to conquer it. His amazing ministry functioned in the framework of the gifts of the Spirit. If what Jesus did, He did because He was God, this leaves us out because we are not gods. If the ministry of Jesus was directed, guided and energized by the Holy Spirit, and if we have the same Holy Spirit, then we can do as He said in John 14:12, *Verily, Verily, I say unto you, He that believeth on me, the works that I do shall he do also; and greater works than these shall he do; because I go unto my Father.*

3. OLD TESTAMENT EXAMPLES

If the remarkable men of the Old Testament, such as Moses, David and Daniel, performed their ministry in the framework of the gifts of the Holy Spirit, then our generation can do the works of those men by the same Spirit that motivated them.

If they did their works because they were select individuals which no ordinary Christian could hope to follow, then their story is just a divine record, but if the same power that was in them is available today, then the works that they did, we can do.

4. THE VICTORIOUS CHURCH

A. The infant church emerged from Jerusalem ready to defy pagan Rome with its military might, and atheistic Athens with its philosophical might. It merged to convert the untutored barbarian living in primitive huts and held in the clutches of the awful forces of witchcraft. The early church knew a battle must ensue and it used the gifts of the Spirit to win victories. The modern church of today can do the same works as the first church in Jerusalem and win the same victories.

B. The gifts of the Holy Spirit are called "gifts" to reveal that there is only one way to obtain them. This by no means minimizes their importance. The gifts of the Spirit cannot be *earned* or *merited.*

James 1:17, *Every good and every perfect gift is from above, and cometh down from the Father of lights, with whom is no variableness, neither shadow of turning.*

Although the gifts of the Spirit are called gifts, they are not optional. They are not placed at the disposal of the church on a take-it-or-leave-it basis. They are a necessary part of our fighting gear. They are the weapons of our defense and offense. Without the gifts of the Spirit the church is helpless before the onslaught of the world, the flesh and the devil.

C. The church is either properly equipped for battle or not. Without adequate armor and the know-how to use it, the church will suffer one defeat after another from the enemy. The church must use the gifts of the Spirit.

5. THE BATTLE OF THE SPIRIT

A. The warfare of the church transcends the carnal and the natural (Ephesians 6:10-12; II Corinthians 10:4-5).

The gifts of the Spirit to the believer are what the stone was to David when he slew Goliath.

They are what the jawbone of the ass was to Samson when he slew a thousand men.

For the modern church to seek to win the world from the slavery and bondage of the devil without these instruments of God's power, is like trying to defeat a modern army barehanded, without weapons.

B. Jesus said in Matthew 12:29, *If you wish to take a prey, you must first bind the strong man.* Seeking to take a prey in pagan lands like India, Tibet, China, etc., without using the weapons of our warfare is to suffer a humiliating defeat at the hands of witchcraft, superstition, and heathen religions. When pagan darkness is pushed back, whether overseas in what we consider heathen countries, or in our own country, it is done according to Zechariah 4:6, *Not by might, nor by power, but by my spirit, saith the LORD of hosts.*

6. UNTAPPED POWER

The greatest untapped power on the face of this earth is *in the church.* The greatest unused strength in the world lays dormant in the church. If there is a sleeping giant that could change this world it is the *church of Jesus Christ.* It must awake to the challenge of the Great Commission clothed in the armor of God's *revelation power* and *inspiration.* It can then march to unprecedented victories and glories for our Lord Jesus Christ.

SYLLABUS

WORLD HARVEST SCHOOL OF CONTINUOUS LEARNING

STUDY: THE GIFTS AND MINISTRIES OF THE HOLY SPIRIT

LESSON 4

WHAT ARE THE GIFTS?

INTRODUCTION:

Although spiritual gifts are discernable through the entire Bible, the Holy Spirit in I Corinthians 12, through the Apostle Paul, gives us names and explanations concerning the gifts of the Holy Spirit and the church of Jesus Christ.

READING:

I Corinthians 12:1, 4-11, *Now concerning spiritual gifts, brethren, I would not have you ignorant.*

v. 4, *Now there are diversities of gifts, but the same Spirit.*

v. 5, *And there are differences of administrations, but the same Lord.*

v. 6, *And there are diversities of operations, but it is the same God which worketh all in all.*

v. 7, *But the manifestation of the Spirit is given to every man to profit withal.*

v. 8, *For to one is given by the Spirit the word of wisdom; to another the word of knowledge by the same Spirit;*

v. 9, *To another faith by the same Spirit; to another the gifts of healing by the same Spirit;*

v. 10, *To another the working of miracles; to another prophecy; to another discerning of spirits; to another divers kinds of tongues; to another the interpretation of tongues:*

v. 11, *But all these worketh that one and the selfsame Spirit, dividing to every man severally as he will.*

1. **THE GIFTS ARE FROM THE HOLY SPIRIT**

   I was born and reared in the Full Gospel movement when the world impact of it was phenomenal. Not only did I see this impact over the nation of America, but visited it in over one hundred nations of the world.

The gifts operating in you do not prove your spirituality. In many minds, a generation ago, the baptism of the Holy Spirit and gifts of the Spirit were something like the "frosting on the cake." It proved to them that the Pentecostal people were better than the Baptists, Methodists or Catholics. They felt that the Holy Spirit baptism made them more holy than the Presbyterians, more sanctified than the Methodists, and above all, made them God's favorites.

This is where the traditional Pentecostal people missed the true meaning of the baptism in the Holy Ghost and the gifts of the Spirit. They are the weapons of our warfare and not a superfluous extra added to some and not to others.

2. THE GIFTS ARE ALL SUPERNATURAL

They signified a breakthrough of the omnipotence, omnipresence and omniscience of the Third Person of the Trinity; and they are the same today.

3. THE GIFTS ARE FOR THE TOTAL CHURCH BODY

They flow in the church as part of the church. Gifts of the Spirit do not prove spirituality or dedication. People with gifts are not necessarily better than others.

4. THE GIFTS OF THE SPIRIT ARE THE WEAPONS OF OUR WARFARE

A. If an army went out to battle with no training or weapons, it would lose. If soldiers went out to battle without understanding their equipment, they would still lose. Any defeat that the church suffers is because it either does not have the weapons of its warfare, or it does not understand the equipment which it has to fight its battles.

B. These weapons include:
   1) The blood of Jesus
   2) The Word of God
   3) The name of Jesus

C. Our battle is in the spiritual world. The Word of God in Ephesians 6:12 specifically says, *For we wrestle not against flesh and blood, but against principalities, against powers, against the rulers of the darkness of this world, against spiritual wickedness in high places.*

Immediately we realize that the more weapons of warfare we possess and the better we know how to utilize them, the more successful we will be in battle.

D. These weapons have never left the church.

5. THE CONFIRMATION OF HISTORY

A. If a person studies the great revivals of history and analyzes them, he will discover these tremendous weapons of our warfare in action at the time of these great victories.

B. Personally, I have seen the entire nation of the Philippines move toward God. It began and was perpetuated by the gifts of the Spirit, especially the gift of healing being in operation.

Therefore, the hope of great revival is the moving and the functioning of these gifts of the Holy Spirit, which beyond doubt are the weapons of our warfare.

6. BE NOT IGNORANT

A. I Corinthians 12:1, *Now concerning spiritual gifts, brethren, I would not have you ignorant.*

Notice the words are directed to brethren. The gifts of the Spirit are only for believers in Jesus Christ.

When Jesus was talking to His disciples, knowing that He would soon face crucifixion and later would ascend into heaven to be with the Father, He spoke solemn words to them. He promised that He would pray to the Father that He would give them another Comforter.

John 14:16-17, *. . .another Comforter, that he may abide with you for ever;*

v. 17, *Even the Spirit of truth; whom the world cannot receive, because it seeth him not, neither knoweth him: but ye know him; for he dwelleth with you, and shall be in you.*

B. The Holy Spirit commanded the church not to be ignorant concerning spiritual gifts. It is most amazing that when God says do not be ignorant we proceed to be more ignorant about that than we do other things. To overcome this ignorance we must study all available information and in prayer seek to comprehend the total truth regarding the gifts of the Spirit.

C. The world is dying of ignorance.

1) The medical world is ignorant of how to cure cancer, heart attacks and AIDS.

2) The Third World is ignorant of the importance of cleanliness and sanitation.

3) Today, much of the Christian world is ignorant of truth and the need to use their spiritual gifts.

SYLLABUS

WORLD HARVEST SCHOOL OF CONTINUOUS LEARNING

STUDY: THE GIFTS AND MINISTRIES OF THE HOLY SPIRIT

LESSON 5

EXPOSITION ON I CORINTHIANS 12

INTRODUCTION:

The gifts of the Spirit stand on two great foundations: unity and love.

READING:

I Corinthians 12:1,   *Now concerning spiritual gifts, brethren, I would not have you ignorant.*

1. **THE UNITY OF THE GIFTS OF THE SPIRIT**

   A. Verse 4,   *Now there are diversities of gifts, but the same Spirit.* The gifts vary from divine revelation, to resplendent and amazing power, to the glorious inspiration of prophecy. The Bible says though there are diversities of gifts, there is the *sameness of spirit.* There is no difference in the spirit that proceeds from the gift of the word of wisdom or that proceeds from the gift of interpretation of tongues. This is very important.

   B. Verse 5,   *And there are differences of administrations, but the same Lord.* In administration we have degrees of leadership. The gift of the word of wisdom is the functioning of an apostle or prophet. The gift of prophecy may function in any lay member of the church. It is the same Lord Jesus Christ in command whether it is changing a nation or blessing one person. Whether it be a great work with thousands being born again or a small work with one person converted, it is the same Lord administering His power.

   C. Verse 6,   *And there are diversities of operation, but it is the same God which worketh all in all.* Diversities of operations means *of working to accomplish things* (AMP). In the powerful functioning of the church of Christ there are operations which cost millions of dollars and there are other operations that cost little or

19

nothing, but it is the same God who is working. This is teaching us the unity of the Body of Christ and the respect that we must have one for another. Whatever the operation with which God charges us, whether it be house-to-house visitation, passing out tracts, or moving an entire nation by preaching on television, it is His work and it is the same God who works all in all. We are not to be jealous one of the other. We are all to perform together in Christ.

D. Verse 7, *But the manifestation of the Spirit is given to every man to profit withal.* We have three key words in this sentence. One is *manifestation;* then, *every man;* and the third one, *profit.* These are three tremendous truths to know.

1) "Manifestation" means for one or more of the nine gifts to be apparent in your life, it is the demonstration of a gift of the Spirit.

2) Then they are given to "every man." This must be accentuated because so many of us eliminate ourselves from the truly great things of God. I maintain that every man means every man. Each person in any congregation can look up to God for manifestation of the gifts of the Spirit in his life. We cannot say this too strongly. We must not look for our weaknesses and difficulties and say the gifts of the Spirit are not for us. The Bible says *every man.*

3) The third is "profit." There is spiritual profit, ". . .common good" (AMP), to every individual who manifests the gifts of the Spirit. If one is poor in spirit and leans on the good things of God, then a move into the gifts of the Spirit will bring him the tremendous profits which belong to those who manifest the gifts of the Spirit.

2. INVOLVING EVERY MAN

A. Verse 11, *All these worketh that one and the selfsame Spirit, dividing to every man severally as He will.* We have here the selfsame Spirit, or the Holy Spirit, working in all the divine aspects of the gifts of the Spirit. The great truth is, He is *dividing to every man individually exactly as He chooses* (AMP). It concludes by saying, *as he will.* The Holy Spirit is the One who makes the ultimate decisions about our lives. The nearer we get to Him and to His divine directions, the more the gifts of the Spirit will function in our lives and the church.

B. Verse 12, *For as the body is one, and hath many members, and all the members of that one body, being many, are one body: so also is Christ.* We are bound together by the blood of Jesus, not by denominations or doctrines.

C. Verse 13, *For by one Spirit are we all baptized into one body, whether we be Jews or Gentiles, whether we be bond or free; and have been all made to drink into one Spirit.* The Body of Christ is made up of people of varied backgrounds and nationalities. The Holy Spirit is the uniting force creating a colossal body through which the power of God flows throughout the whole world.

3. GOD MAKES YOU WHAT YOU ARE; ALL BODY PARTS ARE IMPORTANT

Verse 14-20, *For the body is not one member, but many.*

Verses 15, *If the foot shall say, Because I am not the hand, I am not of the body; is it therefore not of the body?*

v. 16, *And if the ear shall say, Because I am not the eye, I am not of the body; is it therefore not of the body?*

v. 17, *If the whole body were an eye, where were the hearing? If the whole were hearing, where were the smelling?*

v. 18, *But now hath God set the members every one of them in the body, as it hath pleased him.*

v. 19, *And if they were all one member, where were the body?*

v. 20, *But now are they many members, yet but one body.*

The Lord chooses your place in the body. If you are a businessman, support those around you; If you are a housewife, touch and bless your family. If you are a minister, be strong and effective in your calling.

4. TAKE CARE OF THE BODY

Verses 21-27, *And the eye cannot say unto the hand, I have no need of thee: nor again the head to the feet, I have no need of you.*

v. 22, *Nay, much more those members of the body, which seem to be more feeble, are necessary:*

v. 23, *And those members of the body, which we think to be less honourable, upon these we bestow more abundant honour; and our uncomely parts have more abundant comeliness.*

v. 24, *For our comely parts have no need: but God hath tempered the body together, having given more abundant honour to that part which lacked:*

v. 25,   *That there should be no schism in the body; but that the members should have the same care one for another.*

v. 26,   *And whether one member suffer, all the members suffer with it; or one member be honoured, all the members rejoice with it.*

v. 27,   *Now ye are the body of Christ, and members in particular.*

The power of God will operate when the members of the body really care for each other creating a spiritual relationship among God's people.

5. GOD GIVES GIFTS TO THE CHURCH

Verse 28-31,   *And God hath set some in the church, first apostles, secondarily prophets, thirdly teachers, after that miracles, then gifts of healings, helps, governments, diversities of tongues.*

v. 29,   *Are all apostles? are all prophets? are all teachers? are all workers of miracles?*

v. 30,   *Have all the gifts of healing? do all speak with tongues? do all interpret?*

v. 31,   *But covet earnestly the best gifts: and yet shew I unto you a more excellent way.*

Even as the Church is made up of many members with varied gifts and from various backgrounds, the ministry, as well, is divided among several people with different ministries. They must also work together to edify and instruct the body of Christ.

WORLD HARVEST SCHOOL OF CONTINUOUS LEARNING

STUDY: THE GIFTS AND MINISTRIES OF THE HOLY SPIRIT

LESSON 6

THE CHARISMATIC RENEWAL

INTRODUCTION:

Possibly the most amazing spiritual revolution since the reformation is taking place in the world at this moment.

A new power has evidenced itself among Christians. Unlimited by authority, this following, made up of many backgrounds of people, is marching toward New Testament truth and experience.

A most misunderstood segment of the Christian church, the Pentecostals, has become a powerful force throughout the world. They are known as members of "the charismatic renewal." Multitudes of Catholics, Episcopalians, Lutherans, Methodists, Baptists and other traditional churches, have received the baptism of the Holy Spirit as on the day of Pentecost and speaking with tongues.

It is amazing that when Catholics began to move into spiritual realities they bypassed the fundamental and orthodox denominations and entered the ranks of Pentecostal churches.

Multitudes in the charismatic renewal meet in college classrooms, private homes or borrowed halls to worship and exercise the gifts of the Spirit. Large new churches have sprung up all over—churches that are outdistancing mainline denominations in membership, educational facilities, and ongoing growth.

READING:

Acts 2:17, *And it shall come to pass in the last days, saith God, I will pour out of my Spirit upon all flesh: and your sons and your daughters shall prophesy, and your young men shall see visions, and your old men shall dream dreams.*

1. THE EXPERIENCE

By and large, the appearance of these spirit-filled groups of believers, is looked upon as a fulfillment of Acts 2:17.

The charismatic communtiy of today appears to agree substantially with these premises:

A. At salvation the living Christ comes to dwell in the spirit of man by His Holy Spirit.

B. At the infilling or baptism of the Holy Spirit, the indwelling Spirit of Christ is able to rule in the minds and the bodies of individuals. A key part of this experience is the releasing of the means of expression. The very heart and center of our ego-centered lives, our means of expression, our means of thought, and our means of verbalizing, release the power of the indwelling Jesus Christ. This then becomes a cornerstone of our faith.

2. THE DANGERS

A. Overly exalting an experience.

B. Neglecting the house of God for worship.

C. Refusing to take advice from God's appointed leaders.

3. THE FRUIT OF CHARISMA

The benefits and blessings of the gift:

A. A love for the Word of God not experienced before.

B. A stewardship unknown before.

C. An ability to face up to sins and confess them.

D. A tremendous growth in compassion for others.

E. A new ministry and service to people in the field of counseling.

F. A praising and singing congregation.

G. Many outstanding experiences in healing.

WORLD HARVEST SCHOOL OF CONTINUOUS LEARNING

STUDY: THE GIFTS AND MINISTRIES OF THE HOLY SPIRIT

LESSON 7

CHARISMA THROUGH THE CENTURIES

INTRODUCTION:

Current history is better understood in the perspective of the related past. The gifts of the Spirit, including speaking in tongues, have appeared and reappeared in the Church from its conception. They have been manifested in every branch of Christendom today.

READING:

Acts 2:37-39, *Now when they heard this, they were pricked in their heart, and said unto Peter and to the rest of the apostles, Men and brethren, what shall we do?*

v. 38, *Then Peter said unto them, Repent, and be baptized every one of you in the name of Jesus Christ for the remission of sins, and ye shall receive the gift of the Holy Ghost.*

v. 39, *For the promise is unto you, and to your children, and to all that are afar off, even as many as the Lord our God shall call.*

1. **IN HISTORY**

    A. Dr. Philip Schaff, the well-known church historian, in his *History of the Apostolic Church,* Book 1, sec. 55 writes: "The speaking with tongues, however, was not confined to the Day of Pentecost. Together with the other extraordinary spiritual gifts which distinguished this age above the succeeding periods of more quiet and natural development, this gift also, though to be sure in a modified form, perpetuated itself in the apostolic church. We find traces of it still in the second and third centuries."

    B. Irenaeus (115 to 202 A.D.) was a pupil of Polycarp, who was a disciple of the Apostle John. He wrote in his book, *Against Heresies,* Book V: "In like manner do we also hear many brethren in the church who possess prophetic gifts and who through the Spirit speak all kinds of languages, and bring to mysteries of God, whom also the apostles term spiritual."

C. The Latin church father, Tertullian (160 to 220 A.D.), writing against Marcion, said: "Let Marcion then exhibit, as gifts of his god, some prophets, such as have not spoken by human sense, but with the Spirit of God, such as have predicted things to come, and have made manifest the secrets of the heart; let him produce a psalm, a vision, a prayer—only let it be by the Spirit, in an ecstasy, that is, in a rapture, whenever an interpretation of tongues has occurred to him. . .Now all these signs (or spiritual gifts) are forthcoming from my side without any difficulty, and they agree, too, with the rules, and the dispensations, and the instructions of the Creator. . ." *Smith's of the Dictionary Bible* vol. 4, page 3310.

D. St. Pachomius (292-346), the Egyptian founder of the first Christian monastery, is said to have enjoyed the use of the Greek and Latin languages which he sometimes miraculously spoke, having never learned them. This gift was given to him at times after special prayer for the power to meet an immediate need. *Giver of the Saints,* A. Butler, published 1756.

E. The history of the Waldneses in the 12th century reveals not only a devotion to Bible reading and a desire to follow the primitive purity of the New Testament church, but also that both healing and speaking in unknown languages were experienced from time to time in their midst. Alexandria Mockie—*Gift of Tongues,* page 27.

F. John Calvin (1509-1564), wrote in his commentary of *The Epistles of Paul the Apostle to the Corinthians*:

"There are at present great theologians, who declaim against them with furious zeal. As it is certain, that the Holy Spirit has here honored the use of tongues with never-dying praise, we may very readily gather, what is the kind of spirit that actuates those reformers, who level as many reproaches as they can against the pursuit of them." This particular comment is in reference to a verse in I Corinthians, chapter 14: *I would that ye all spake with tongues. . .*

G. Martin Luther is mentioned in Souer's *History of the Christian Church,* vol. 3, page 206.

"Dr. Martin Luther was a prophet, evangelist, speaker in tongues and interpreter, in one person, endowed with all the gifts of the Holy Spirit."

H. Dwight L. Moody. Here are a few quotations from page 402, *Trials and Triumphs of Faith,* (1875 edition), by the Rev. R. Boyd, D.D. (Baptist), who was a very intimate friend of the famous evangelist: "When I got to the rooms of the Young Men's Christian Association (Victoria Hall, London), I found the meeting on fire. The young men were speaking with tongues and prophesying. What on earth did it mean? Only that Moody has been addressing them that afternoon! What manner of man is this? I cannot describe Moody's great meeting: I can only say that the people of Sunderland warmly supported the movement, in spite of their local spiritual advisors."

I. John Wesley said in his journal that "people fell under a strange power and he could not bring them around. They laid them on wagons and took them home and some of them were cackling like geese."

J. At the dawn of the 20th century the Holy Spirit was poured out in abundance. It centered in the metropolis of Los Angeles and soon spread around the entire earth.

WORLD HARVEST SCHOOL OF CONTINUOUS LEARNING

STUDY: THE GIFTS AND MINISTRIES OF THE HOLY SPIRIT

LESSON 8

THE CHURCH OPERATING IN UNITY AND LOVE

INTRODUCTION:

The gifts of the Spirit will not function long without unity. The Church was born in unity and it can only be great when in unity. God always deals with us through our spirit, then our spirit communicates with our mind, emotions and willpower.

READING:

I Corinthians 12:12, *For as the body is one, and hath many members, and all the members of that one body, being many, are one body: so also is Christ.*

1. **THERE IS POWER IN UNITY**

   A. Even a small group of people can build a cathedral if their unity is strong.

   B. I Corinthians 12:13, *For by one Spirit are we all baptized into one body, whether we be Jews or Gentiles, whether we be bond or free; and have been all made to drink into one Spirit.*

   Being a member of a denomination does not necessarily make us a part of the body of Christ. We are in the body because God put us in the body.

2. **GOD NEEDS ALL KINDS OF PEOPLE**

   A. Verse 14, *For the body is not one member, but many.*

   A body has both eyes, a nose, and ears. In the body of Christ, God needs the Salvation Army, as well as the Episcopalians, etc.

   B. I Corinthians 12:21, *The eye cannot say unto the hand, I have no need of thee: nor again the head to the feet, I have no need of you.*

   To God we are all important.

C. Be careful not to judge or quarrel with other sections of the body.

3. THE CHURCH PERFECTED IN SUFFERING

Verse 26, *And whether one member suffer, all the members suffer with it. . .*

I remember in Rome, right after World War II, meeting a pastor who had been in jail seventeen times for preaching on the street. His secretary had been in jail ten times for the same thing. Their church went underground and suffered great persecution during the reign of Mussolini. Now they have a wonderful church and own their own radio station. But they suffered, and others in the body suffered with them even though they were not imprisoned.

4. COVET THE GIFTS

Verse 31, *. . .covet earnestly the best gifts. . .*

Previous verses speak of the diversity of the body of Christ, emphasizing that not all have the same gifts. To receive spiritual gifts you must earnestly desire them and seek after them.

5. THE MORE EXCELLENT WAY—I CORINTHIANS 13

A. The first great footing upon which the gifts of the Spirit must be based is unity. The second footing is love.

B. Power without love can be disastrous.

C. Gifts without love are simply noise.

I Corinthians 13:1-3, *Though I speak with the tongues of men and of angels, and have not charity, I am become as sounding brass, or a tinkling cymbal.*

v. 2, *And though I have the gift of prophecy, and understand all mysteries, and all knowledge; and though I have all faith, so that I could remove mountains, and have not charity, I am nothing.*

v. 3, *And though I bestow all my goods to feed the poor, and though I give my body to be burned, and have not charity, it profiteth me nothing.*

D. Description of love.

Verses 4-13, *Charity suffereth long, and is kind; charity envieth not; charity vaunteth not itself, is not puffed up,*

v. 5,   *Doth not behave itself unseemly, seeketh not her own, is not easily provoked, thinketh no evil;*

v. 6,   *Rejoiceth not in inquity, but rejoiceth in the truth;*

v. 7,   *Beareth all things, believeth all things, hopeth all things, endureth all things.*

v. 8,   *Charity never faileth: but whether there be prophecies, they shall fail; whether there be tongues, they shall cease; whether there be knowledge, it shall vanish away.*

v. 9,   *For we know in part, and we prophesy in part.*

v. 10,   *But when that which is perfect is come, then that which is in part shall be done away.*

v. 11,   *When I was a child, I spake as a child, I understood as a child, I thought as a child: but when I became a man, I put away childish things.*

v. 12,   *For now we see through a glass, darkly; but then face to face: now I know in part; but then shall I know even as also I am known.*

v. 13,   *And now abideth faith, hope, charity, these three; but the greatest of these is charity.*

Love—

1)   Is patient and kind; is not jealous;
2)   Is not boastful (does not brag); is not arrogant;
3)   Is not rude (unmannerly); does not insist on its own way; is not self-seeking; is not touchy or resentful.
4)   Rejoices when right and truth prevail.
5)   Is hopeful
6)   Endures without weakening; believes the best,
7)   Never fails
8)   Matures. . .
9)   Is greater than faith and hope

SYLLABUS

WORLD HARVEST SCHOOL OF CONTINUOUS LEARNING

STUDY: THE GIFTS AND MINISTRIES OF THE HOLY SPIRIT

LESSON 9

A DEFINITION OF THE NINE GIFTS OF THE HOLY SPIRIT

INTRODUCTION:

You will notice that there are nine gifts of the Spirit listed. This is 3 x 3. Three is the number of divine perfection. When it is multiplied by three, it becomes perfection times perfection. This is a tremendous display of completeness, finality and unity.

READING:

I Corinthians 12:8-11, *For to one is given by the Spirit the word of wisdom; to another the word of knowledge by the same Spirit;*

v. 9, *To another faith by the same Spirit; to another the gifts of healing by the same Spirit;*

v. 10, *To another the working of miracles; to another prophecy; to another discerning of spirits; to another divers kinds of tongues; to another the interpretation of tongues.*

v. 11, *But all these worketh that one and the selfsame Spirit, dividing to every man severally as he will.*

1. **THE GIFTS ARE SUPERNATURAL**

    A. Everyone of these gifts is supernatural. Paul shows clearly in verse 11 that these gifts are miraculously bestowed. These gifts cannot be acquired by the human mind or emotions. These gifts cannot be attained either by labor or holiness. We must emphasize the word "gift" and believe that it is bestowed by the wisdom and power of the Holy Ghost.

    B. For example, King Solomon did not possess the gift of the word of wisdom. He requested of God an enlarged brain in order to govern a nation and God gave it to him. He did not use it in a spiritual capacity as the gifts of the Spirit are used, but used it to build up his nation (see II Chronicles 1:10-12).

2. **THREE CATEGORIES OF GIFTS**

In defining the gifts, we first place them in their *proper* categories. They naturally and spiritually divide themselves into three primary categories:

A. Gifts of revelation: the word of wisdom, the word of knowledge and the discerning of spirits.

B. Gifts of power: faith, the gifts of healing, the working of miracles.

C. Gifts of inspiration: prophecy, divers kinds of tongues and the interpretation of tongues.

3. **A DEFINITION OF CATEGORIES**

These groups are distinguished by what God does in each classification of gifts.

A. In the gifts of revelation, God *reveals* something from heaven to man—something man cannot know any other way.

Matthew 16:17, . . .*flesh and blood hath not revealed it unto thee, but my Father which is in heaven.*

B. In the gifts of power, God *does* something for man. He imparts His own divine energy and abilities.

C. In the gifts of inspiration, God brings blessing to others by edification, exhortation and comfort (I Corinthians 14:3).

Thus we have three natural groupings of gifts. This total of nine gifts is given to the church by the Holy Spirit for a supernatural work.

4. **DEFINING THE GIFTS**

A. The WORD OF WISDOM is the revealing of the prophetic future under the anointing of God.

B. The WORD OF KNOWLEDGE is the revealing of a fact in existence which cannot be seen, heard or revealed naturally. It is in existence, it is a fact, it is knowledge and it is supernaturally revealed by God.

C. The DISCERNING OF SPIRITS has to do with the comprehension of the human spirit as supernaturally revealed by the Holy Ghost.

D. The GIFT OF FAITH is when, without any human effort, God brings to pass a supernatural thing. The Bible defines faith for us:

Hebrews 11:1, *Now faith is the substance of things hoped for, the evidence of things not seen.*

E. The GIFT OF WORKING OF MIRACLES is when, through the human instrument of hands, eyes, mouth or feet, the person supernaturally does something by the divine energy of the Holy Spirit. An Old Testament example would be the incident when Samson killed a lion barehanded (Judges 14:6). A New Testament example would be found in Acts 3 (Peter and the lame man).

F. The GIFTS OF HEALING (the only plural gift) is when God supernaturally heals the sick under the assigned gift ministry.

G. The GIFT OF TONGUES is the ministry of proclaiming in a public meeting a message from God which is not understood by the person giving it.

H. The GIFT OF INTERPRETATION OF TONGUES is when, without any mental facilities operating, the message that has been given in another language is interpreted supernaturally by the Spirit.

I. The GIFT OF PROPHECY is the anointed speaking forth of words of edification, exhortation, or comfort to the church, supernaturally given from God without human thinking.

These are brief definitions of the gifts of the Spirit. Now we will study them one gift at a time.

WORLD HARVEST SCHOOL OF CONTINUOUS LEARNING

STUDY: THE GIFTS AND MINISTRIES OF THE HOLY SPIRIT

LESSON 10

THE GIFT OF PROPHECY

INTRODUCTION:

PROPHECY—God is all powerful. It is an awesome thought that He chooses to use us as channels of His power. One of the ways He does that is through the gift of prophecy.

Words are power—in these lessons on the vocal and inspirational gifts, we witness the remarkable power of words, but words that are anointed and inspired by the Holy Ghost are especially powerful.

Prophecy involves the human will and faith, but does not involve the human intellect.

READING:

I Corinthians 12:10, *. . .to another prophecy. . .*

1. **THE GIFT OF PROPHECY, ONE OF THE GIFTS OF INSPIRATION**

   In this group of studies we have now come to the ecstatic gifts of utterance or the gifts of inspiration. They are completely different from the gifts of revelation where God reveals the future, the present, or the human personality.

   They are very different from the gifts of power where God does a miracle for you by faith or God remarkably heals a person.

   The gift of prophecy is mentioned 22 times in chapters 11-14 of First Corinthians. There is much importance and urgency concerning this gift; it is entirely supernatural in a natural tongue. First Corinthians 12:7 calls the gift a *manifestation of the Spirit of God.* Prophecy is speaking *unto men supernaturally.*

   I Corinthians 14:3, *But he that prophesieth speaketh unto men to edification, and exhortation, and comfort.*

2. DEFINITION OF THE GIFT OF PROPHECY

The word *prophecy* originates from the Hebrew word *naba* meaning, "to flow forth, to spring forth, or to tumble."

A. I Corinthians 14:3, *But he that prophesieth speaketh unto men to edification, and exhortation, and comfort.*

B. We see another of those amazing sets of three.

C. This gift has three divine purposes. Please note that in this gift there is no foretelling of the future; it is the simple gift of prophecy. It does not reach into the gifts of power. Revelation is not the office of a prophet.

4. WHAT THE GIFT OF PROPHECY IS NOT

A. It is not the office of a prophet.

A prophet is a man and not a spiritual gift (Ephesians 4:11). Philip's four daughters prophesied, but were not prophetesses (Acts 21:9).

B. The prophetic office always predicts the future. The gift of prophecy NEVER does (I Corinthians 14:3).

William Smith Bible Dictionary states, "It is certain that neither prescience or prediction are implied by the term in the Hebrew, Greek or English language."

C. Prophecy is not intended for guidance.

No gift can take the place of common sense.
No ministry is to foretell.

D. Prophecy is not regular preaching.

To preach means to proclaim or announce the good news of the gospel. It is the natural mind speaking by the Spirit.

Prophecy is the mind of the Holy Spirit speaking.
Preaching is inspired, but not supernatural.
Prophecy is a supernatural utterance.

E. The possessor of the gift controls prophecy—I Corinthians 14:32.

1) v. 32, *And the spirits of the prophets are subject to the prophets.*
2) The gift is to be regulated. Only three prophecies are allowed in one meeting (v. 27).

3) There are safeguards concerning the use of the gift. Prophecy is not to be despised. We should covet to prophesy (I Thessalonians 5:20).

We must prophesy according to our proportion of faith. If a person prophesies things that do not come to pass, he is speaking beyond his faith.

Romans 12:6, *Having then gifts differing according to the grace that is given to us, whether prophecy, let us prophesy according to the proportion of faith.*

5. EDIFICATION

The gift is primarily to edify the church. It is not directed to unbelievers.

A. Edification, in its root meaning, signifies to erect, to build up, and to strengthen.

I Corinthians 14:4, *He that speaketh in an unknown tongue edifieth himself; but he that prophesieth edifieth the church.*

B. The gifts of inspiration were given to the church by the Holy Spirit to build it up and strengthen it. Certainly this is one of the greatest needs of the present hour.

C. Multitudes of Christians are in great need of having their spiritual lives built up and strengthened. This is no doubt the reason why Paul spoke in tongues more than an entire church; He desired to be "built up" and this is one of the secrets of his amazing strength.

6. EXHORTATION

This is the call to encouragement.

A. The Holy Spirit places the word "exhortation" as the second outreach of the gift of prophecy.

B. Many times I have heard this gift as it exhorts the church to holiness, consecration and separation from the world. This is a spiritual ministry greatly needed in our modern church.

C. There is no element of revelation in New Testament prophecy. It is divided into three areas—edification, exhortation and comfort. In the New Testament, correction comes from preaching the Word and doctrine—not from prophecy. Paul dealt with excess as a teacher, pastor and apostle.

D. Remember, it is not a ministry of criticism. It is not one person's opinion against another. It is a divine operation under the anointing of God, to warn men and women of sin and of shortcomings so they might be ready when Christ returns. This gift can lift a Christian out of depression, or out of his lukewarmness back into the mainstream of the move of God.

7. COMFORT

A. The third and last ministry of the gift of prophecy is comfort. The Greek word means "consolation, in distress, sorrow, persecution, or suffering."

B. It does not take much observation to realize that we live in a world of brokenness— broken lives and broken ambitions.

C. Many churches fail the people who need comfort. We must understand that they do not necessarily need sympathy or pity.

D. The church needs divine comfort where the Holy Spirit brings the healing forces of heaven to people's hearts. As the coming of the Lord nears, this ministry must come forth and comfort the people.

E. Some teachers have intimated that these inspirational gifts are so small that they are almost unnecessary. Even to think such a thing is a reproach against God because he set these spiritual gifts in the church. It is our duty to accept them.

8. HOW DOES THE GIFT OF PROPHECY FUNCTION?

A. When a Christian, in church or before other Christians, speaks under a Holy Spirit anointing in the common language of the people, he is said to be prophesying.

B. The speaker, a man or woman, is anointed, directed, and energized by the Holy Spirit. An example of this is the exhortation Peter gave on the Day of Pentecost. His words were without preparation. His message flowed from his spirit rather than from his mind. If he had sought to prepare such a message, no doubt it would have been impossible.

C. Most often prophecy is used in the church after the delivery of a sermon and the Holy Spirit directly speaks to the people for edifying, exhorting or comforting.

9. LIMITATIONS TO THE GIFT OF PROPHECY

A. It is partial and not complete.

I Corinthians 13:9, *For we know in part, and we prophesy in part.*

B. It is exercised in proportion to faith.

Romans 12:6, *Having then gifts differing according to the grace that is given to us, whether prophecy, let us prophesy according to the proportion of faith.*

C. Its use is limited by its definition.

I Corinthians 14:3, *But he that prophesieth speaketh unto men to edification, and exhortation, and comfort.*

1) Building up (edification).
2) Stirring up (exhortation).
3) Cheering up (comfort).

D. Prophecy is a ministry to the church and is inspirational in character.

10. **PROPHECY IS TO BE JUDGED BY OTHERS WHO ARE PRESENT**

A. I Corinthians 14:29, *Let the prophets speak two or three, and let the other judge.*

B. It can be judged by the Bible.

C. II Peter 1:19, *We have also a more sure word of prophecy; whereunto ye do well that ye take heed, as unto a light that shineth in a dark place, until the day dawn, and the day star arise in your hearts.*

D. Prophecy can be judged by the character of the person speaking.

James 3:8-12, *But the tongue can no man tame; it is an unruly evil, full of deadly poison.*

v. 9, *Therewith bless we God, even the Father; and therewith curse we men, which are made after the similitude of God.*

v. 10, *Out of the same mouth proceedeth blessing and cursing. My brethren, these things ought not so to be.*

v. 11, *Doth a fountain send forth at the same place sweet water and bitter?*

v. 12, *Can the fig tree, my brethren, bear olive berries? either a vine, figs? so can no fountain both yield salt water and fresh.*

E. It can be judged by the gift of discerning of spirits.

I Corinthians 12:10, *To another the working of miracles; to another prophecy; to another discerning of spirits; to another divers kinds of tongues; to another interpretation of tongues.*

F. In the ministry of the gift of prophecy, one is living the broad blessings of the gift, yet within the fixed boundaries of the gifts.

11. **THE GIFT OF PROPHECY AND YOUR PERSONAL RELATIONSHIP TO IT**

A. I Corinthians 14:39, . . .*desire to prophesy*. . .

B. I Corinthians 14:1, . . .*desire spiritual gifts, but especially that you may prophesy*. . .

WORLD HARVEST SCHOOL OF CONTINUOUS LEARNING

STUDY: THE GIFTS AND MINISTRIES OF THE HOLY SPIRIT

LESSON 11

EXPOSITION ON I CORINTHIANS CHAPTER 14

INTRODUCTION:

Do we have the gifts in operation?
Do they function according to the divine pattern?

READING:

I Corinthians 14:1, *Follow after charity, and desire spiritual gifts, but rather that ye may prophesy.*

1. Verse 1—THE WORD "rather" has only to do with the two gifts of prophecy and tongues. Chapter 14 deals with these two gifts of inspiration.

2. Verse 2—GIFT OF TONGUES is for speaking unto God (prayer language).

3. Verse 3—GIFT OF PROPHECY is for speaking to men.

4. Verse 4—TONGUES EDIFY the person speaking.

5. Verse 5—TOTAL CHURCH can participate in this edification (if there is interpretation).

6. Verses 6-13—ILLUSTRATE THE NEED of the gift of interpretation in the open assembly.

   A. Musical instruments must give forth sound and meaning. Music must make sense and sound. I could make a noise on a trumpet, but it would have no meaning. Tongues must be interpreted. They must have meaning.

    B. Verse 10—MANY KINDS OF VOICES—The Greek word used here is *phones*. Oceanographers have now recorded the "voice" of a fish. The mother hen has a voice that her chicks understand. So it is in tongues; the voice is very meaningful. God knows every vibration of tone.

7. Verse 14—TONGUES ALONE in the assembly are unfruitful. We do not just speak into the air. We speak to God.

8. Verse 15—THE BALANCING of the natural and supernatural is necessary.

9. Verse 16—THE UNLEARNED refers to those in the position of being an outsider, or one who is not gifted with tongues.

10. Verse 18—PAUL GIVES HIS PERSONAL TESTIMONY of the use of the gifts.

11. Verse 19—DOES NOT DISPARAGE TONGUES. It proclaims the divine ministry of communication (the need to instruct others). It is a rebuke to selfishness in spiritual places.

12. Verse 20—BRETHREN BE NOT CHILDREN, in your thinking, but in understanding be men.

WORLD HARVEST SCHOOL OF CONTINUOUS LEARNING

STUDY: THE GIFTS AND MINISTRIES OF THE HOLY SPIRIT

LESSON 12

THE GIFT OF TONGUES FOR PUBLIC MINISTRY

INTRODUCTION:

The gift of speaking in tongues is perhaps the most misunderstood of all the gifts of the Spirit.

READING:

I Corinthians 14:2, *For he that speaketh in an unknown tongue speaketh not unto men, but unto God: for no man understandeth him; howbeit in the spirit he speaketh mysteries.*

1. **WHAT IS THE SIGN GIFT OF DIVERS KINDS OF TONGUES?**

   This second gift in the category of inspiration is the gift of divers kinds of tongues.

   A. Speaking with tongues as the Holy Spirit gives utterance is the unique ministry identified only with the church age. Seven of the other gifts, such as the word of wisdom, the word of knowledge, the gifts of healing, and the gift of the working of miracles existed in the Old Testament and during the ministry of Jesus.

      Speaking in tongues began on the Day of Pentecost. It has been identified with the church since its inception (I Corinthians 12:28; I Corinthians 14:21; Isaiah 28:11).

   B. The "sign gift" of divers kinds of tongues is a supernatural utterance from God.

      The "sign gift" of divers kinds of tongues is when God speaks directly to man through man such as on the Day of Pentecost (Acts 2:4-8). The gift is a divine and spiritual communication.

2. THIS SIGN GIFT IS NOT THE SAME AS THE BAPTISM OF THE HOLY SPIRIT

Acts 2:4, *And they were all filled with the Holy Ghost, and began to speak with other tongues, as the Spirit gave them utterance.*

This is a ministry gift, a sign gift, from the Holy Spirit.

3. THE GIFT IS NOT LEARNING A LANGUAGE

The gift of tongues is not the learning of languages.

The person who speaks does not know or understand what he has said. His spirit is speaking to God.

This gift is a special challenge and sign to those who are uninformed.

Acts 2:5-7, 11, *And there were dwelling at Jerusalem Jews, devout men, out of every nation under heaven.*

v. 6, *Now when this was noised abroad, the multitude came together, and were confounded, because that every man heard them speak in his own language.*

v. 7, *And they were all amazed and marvelled, saying one to another, Behold are not all these which speak Galilæans?*

v. 11, . . .*we do hear them speak in our tongues the wonderful works of God.*

4. WHO CAN HAVE THIS SIGN GIFT?

Only Spirit-filled and Spirit-baptized Christians are candidates for this gift. One has to first experience Acts 2:4 and speak in tongues before this church gift can operate. In I Corinthians 14:5, Paul said that he wished everyone to have the gift.

5. THE SPEECH IS TO GOD

I Corinthians 14:2, *For he that speaketh in an unknown tongue speaketh not unto men, but unto God. . .*

It is a verbal or vocal miracle. What a joy it is to speak to God personally and directly.

6. THIS GIFT WAS PROPHESIED BY JESUS

Mark 16:17, *And these signs shall follow them that believe. . .they shall speak with new tongues.*

There is no doubt or ambiguity with Jesus.

7. WHERE DOES THIS GIFT OPERATE?

I Corinthians 14:23, 26, 33, *If therefore the whole church be come together into one place. . .*

v. 26, *How is it then, brethren? when ye come together. . .*

v. 33, *. . .in all churches of the saints.*

God specifically says the vocal gifts of inspiration are designed to edify or build up the church of Jesus Christ.

8. THE GIFT BUILDS UP THE SPEAKER

I Corinthians 14:4, *He that speaketh in an unknown tongue edifieth himself. . .*

A. By word

B. By song

Where to sing: Everywhere, Psalm 96:1-5, *O sing unto the LORD a new song: sing unto the LORD, all the earth.*

v. 2, *Sing unto the LORD, bless his name; shew forth his salvation from day to day.*

v. 3, *Declare his glory among the heathen, his wonders among all people.*

v. 4, *For the LORD is great, and greatly to be praised; he is to be feared above all gods.*

v. 5, *For all the gods of the nations are idols: but the LORD made the heavens.*

The new song: Revelation 5:9-10, *And they sung a new song, saying, Thou art worthy to take the book, and to open the seals thereof: for thou wast slain, and hast redeemed us to God by thy blood out of every kindred, and tongue, and people, and nation;*

v. 10, *And hast made us unto our God kings and priests: and we shall reign on the earth.*

When to sing: Always, Ephesians 5:19-20, *Speaking to yourselves in psalms and hymns and spiritual songs, singing and making melody in your heart to the Lord;*

v. 20, *Giving thanks always for all things unto God and the Father in the name of our Lord Jesus Christ.*

Sing to your problems: Colossians 3:16, *Let the word of Christ dwell in you richly in all wisdom; teaching and admonishing one another in psalms and hymns and spiritual songs, singing with grace in your hearts to the Lord.*

Spiritual songs: Ephesians 5:19, *Speaking to yourselves in psalms and hymns and spiritual songs, singing and making melody in your heart to the Lord.*

The song of the Lord: Psalm 137:4, *How shall we sing the LORD's song in a strange land?*

9. THE SPEAKERS IN TONGUES SHOULD SEEK THE SECOND GIFT OF INTERPRETATION

The person who speaks in an unknown tongue may also be granted the second gift of interpretation.

I Corinthians 14:13, *Wherefore let him that speaketh in an unknown tongue pray that he may interpret.*

10. IT IS A GIFT FROM THE SPIRIT AND NOT FROM THE SOUL

I Corinthians 14:14, *For if I pray in an unknown tongue, my spirit prayeth, but my understanding is unfruitful.*

This gift flows from the spirit and not the mind.

11. TONGUES ARE A SIGN TO THE SINNER

I Corinthians 14:22, *Wherefore tongues are for a sign, not to them that believe, but to them that believe not: but prophesying serveth not for them that believe not, but for them which believe.*

12. TONGUES WITHOUT INTERPRETATION ARE FORBIDDEN IN CHURCH SERVICES

I Corinthians 14:28, *But if there be no interpreter, let him keep silence in the church; and let him speak to himself, and to God.*

13. CAN THIS GIFT BE REGULATED?

It must be kept decent and in order by leadership.

I Corinthians 14:29-32, *Let the prophets speak two or three, and let the other judge.*

v. 30, *If any thing be revealed to another that sitteth by, let the first hold his peace.*

v. 31, *For ye may all prophesy one by one, that all may learn, and all may be comforted.*

v. 32, *And the spirits of the prophets are subject to the prophets.*

14. THIS GIFT IS LIMITED IN USE

I Corinthians 14:27, *If any man speak in an unknown tongue, let it be by two, or at the most by three, and that by course; and let one interpret.*

The Holy Spirit is showing that He can get His message across in two or three messages in tongues. The reason for this is found in I Corinthians 14:33, *For God is not the author of confusion, but of peace, as in all churches of the saints.*

15. CHURCH LEADERS MUST NOT FORBID THIS GIFT

I Corinthians 14:39, *Wherefore, brethren, covet to prophesy, and forbid not to speak with tongues.*

Paul said in I Corinthians 14:5, *I would that ye all spake with tongues. . .*

Is it not normal for the supernatural to overrule the natural when operating in the gifts of the Holy Spirit? God has you in control.

16. THIS GIFT CAN BE NEGLECTED

It can be stiffened to death. It can lie dormant and lifeless. God does not compel the use of any gift from heaven.

I Timothy 4:14, *Neglect not the gift that is in thee, which was given thee by prophecy, with the laying on of the hands of the presbytery.*

17. WHEN WILL TONGUES CEASE?

I Corinthians 13:8-10, . . .*whether there be tongues, they shall cease; whether there be knowledge, it shall vanish away.*

v. 9, *For we know in part, and we prophesy in part.*

v. 10, *But when that which is perfect is come, then that which is in part shall be done away.*

The Holy Spirit is particularly identified with the church. Has the church age ended? There is no Bible intimation of a change from the day the church was born until the rapture.

Tongues will cease at the end of this age at the same time when knowledge shall vanish and the church will be in heaven with our Lord.

18. WHY WILL TONGUES CEASE?

A. In heaven we will no longer need the Holy Spirit to guide us into truth. We will speak the same language as Jesus.

I Corinthians 13:12, *For now we see through a glass, darkly; but then face to face: now I know in part; but then shall I know even as also I am known.*

B. We will no longer need tongues as a sign to the unbelievers. There will be no unbelievers.

I Corinthians 14:22, *Wherefore tongues are for a sign, not to them that believe, but to them that believe not. . .*

C. We will no longer need unknown tongues to glorify God in Heaven.

Revelation 19:1-2a, 6b, *And after these things I heard a great voice of much people in heaven, saying, Alleluia; Salvation, and glory, and honour, and power, unto the Lord our God:*

v. 2a, *For true and righteous are his judgments:*

v. 6b, *Alleluia: for the Lord God omnipotent reigneth.*

D. We will no longer need tongues to edify ourselves.

I Corinthians 14:4, *He that speaketh in an unknown tongue edifieth himself. . .*

19. WHY YOU SHOULD CONSISTENTLY SPEAK IN TONGUES

A. It is the evidence of the infilling of the Holy Spirit.

1) Acts 2:4, *And they were all filled with the Holy Ghost, and began to speak with other tongues, as the Spirit gave them utterance.*

2) Acts 10:44-46a, *While Peter yet spake these words, the Holy Ghost fell on all them which heard the word.*

v. 45, *And they of the circumcision which believed were astonished, as many as came with Peter, because that on the Gentiles also was poured out the gift of the Holy Ghost.*

v. 46, *For they heard them speak with tongues, and magnify God. . .*

3) Acts 19:1-6, *And it came to pass, that, while Apollos was at Corinth, Paul having passed through the upper coasts came to Ephesus: and finding certain disciples,*

v. 2, *He said unto them, Have ye received the Holy Ghost since ye believed? And they said unto him, We have not so much as heard whether there be any Holy Ghost.*

v. 3, *And he said unto them, Unto what then were ye baptized? And they said, Unto John's baptism.*

v. 4, *Then said Paul, John verily baptized with the baptism of repentance, saying unto the people, that they should believe on him which should come after him, that is, on Christ Jesus.*

v. 5, *When they heard this, they were baptized in the name of the Lord Jesus.*

v. 6, *And when Paul had laid his hands upon them, the Holy Ghost came on them; and they spake with tongues, and prophesied.*

B. It is a prayer language for speaking supernaturally to God.

I Corinthians 14:2, *. . .speaketh not unto men, but unto God. . .*

C. It is to magnify God.

Acts 10:46, *For they heard them speak with tongues, and magnify God. . .*

D. It is to build up spiritual strength in yourself.

We edify ourselves. I Corinthians 14:4, *He that speaketh in an unknown tongue edifieth himself; but he that prophesieth edifieth the church.*

E. It helps us possess gladness in singing.

I Corinthians 14:15, *. . .I will sing with the spirit. . .*

F. It is a source of intercessory prayer.

Romans 8:26, *. . .the spirit itself maketh intercession for us with groanings. . .*

G. It is a source of spiritual refreshing.

Isaiah 28:12, *. . .this is the refreshing. . .*

H. It is a repository of profit.

I Corinthians 12:7, *but the manifestation of the Spirit is given to every man to profit withal. . .*

47

WORLD HARVEST SCHOOL OF CONTINUOUS LEARNING

STUDY: THE GIFTS AND MINISTRIES OF THE HOLY SPIRIT

LESSON 13

GIFT OF THE INTERPRETATION OF TONGUES

INTRODUCTION:

The gift of the interpretation of tongues is the supernatural showing forth by the Spirit the meaning of an utterance spoken by a person in a language which he does not understand.

READING:

I Corinthians 12:10b, *. . .to another the interpretation of tongues.*

1. **THE PURPOSE OF THE GIFT OF INTERPRETATION**

   The purpose of this gift is to render the message from Christ, which has been given in an unintelligible tongue, intelligible to those present.

2. **THE BODY MINISTRY OF THIS GIFT**

   The interpretation of tongues is to edify the church. We know this because this gift functions with its sister gift of speaking in tongues.

   I Corinthians 14:4-5, *He that speaketh in an unknown tongue edifieth himself; but he that prophesieth edifieth the church.*

   v. 5, *I would that ye all spake with tongues, but rather that ye prophesied: for greater is he that prophesieth than he that speaketh with tongues, except he interpret, that the church may receive edifying.*

3. **THIS GIFT EXALTS THE LORD JESUS CHRIST**

   It is the functioning of the miracle which can be seen easily by the unbeliever and causes amazement to him as witnessed on the Day of Pentecost when the church was born.

Acts 2:1-4,   *And when the day of Pentecost was fully come, they were all with one accord in one place.*

v. 2,   *And suddenly there came a sound from heaven as of a rushing mighty wind, and it filled all the house where they were sitting.*

v. 3,   *And there appeared unto them cloven tongues like as of fire, and it sat upon each of them.*

v. 4,   *And they were all filled with the Holy Ghost, and began to speak with other tongues, as the Spirit gave them utterance.*

4.   NOT A TRANSLATION

The message in tongues might be long and the interpretation of tongues might be short or it could be vice versa.

5.   NOT AN OPERATION OF THE HUMAN MIND

It is a functioning of the Holy Spirit through the mind. The interpreter does not understand the language of the tongue he is interpreting. His mental faculties are not part of the message.

6.   WHEN THERE IS NO INTERPRETATION

A.   It is because there is no one present with the gift of interpretation.

B.   The person is simply magnifying God and there is no public interpretation of the message necessary.

C.   I have heard a foreign person speak in tongues. The message was in English and the interpretation was in the native tongue of those present.

7.   TWO KINDS OF INTERPRETATION OF TONGUES

A.   In words spoken inspirationally.

B.   In the form of a vision where a person sees the thing about which he is speaking.

8.   HOW THE INTERPRETATION OF TONGUES COMES

The interpreter normally receives only one or two words and as he speaks these the remaining part of the message opens up a few words at a time. The interpreter has no thought in mind as to what the Spirit has to say. It comes forth from his spirit and not from his mind.

A. A tremendous illustration of the fruit of this gift took place when I preached in Washington D.C. After my sermon, there was a message in tongues and a brother interpreted. When they had finished, a young man from the back of the building walked to the front and spoke a foreign language to the one who gave the message. The brother answered, "I'm sorry sir, I do not understand any other language. I am a car salesman here in Washington."

The man replied, "But you spoke my language beautifully. I am a Persian and I am here selling Persian carpets and you spoke my language and told me that I must get right with God and that I must find God now."

The brother answered, "No, that was the Spirit that spoke to you and it was God. It was not me." To his surprise neither of the two men spoke or understood his language.

I stood there while this young man knelt at the altar and gave his heart to the Lord Jesus Christ.

B. Illustration: How I received this gift.

I was asked to pastor the South Bend Tabernacle. I felt led of God to accept the pastorate. However, I reminded God that I believed every pastor must have the spiritual gift of interpreting tongues. Otherwise, how could he pastor a charismatic church? This gift I had never had. Almost reluctantly I went to the church. On the first Sunday a lady gave a message in tongues. Instantly the gift was born in my heart. I had the interpretation. The gift was received.

Surely the gifts of the Spirit are the weapons of our warfare.

LESSON 14

THE GIFT OF THE WORD OF WISDOM

INTRODUCTION:

In the category of revelation gifts, God supernaturally reveals through a man or woman that which their minds cannot conceive, their ears have not heard, their eyes have not seen. The first of these is the gift of the word of wisdom.

READING:

I Corinthians 12:8, *For to one is given by the Spirit the word of wisdom. . .*

1. **WHAT THE GIFT IS NOT**

   The gift of the word of wisdom is not that a person is brilliant or that he has academic success in any given subject. In fact, the gift has nothing to do with worldly wisdom.

2. **IT IS A SUPERNATURAL REVELATION**

   The gift of the word of wisdom is supernatural revelation of the divine purposes of God in Christ, communicated by the Holy Spirit to the church through a believer. This gift unveils in part the purposes of God on the earth. Paul explained it this way in I Corinthians 2:7, *But we speak the wisdom of God in a mystery, even the hidden wisdom, which God ordained before the world unto our glory.*

3. **IT IS A FRAGMENT OF GOD'S WISDOM**

   A. **The student** must remember that the name of this gift is "word of wisdom." It is a fragment of the total wisdom of God, as a word is a fragment of a sentence. We receive a fragment of His wisdom. This means the word of wisdom is a part and portion of the great omniscience of God.

B. God is all wise. God knows the total future. When He conveys to the Church through one of His servants something He is going to do, He has made that person wise in that one matter. However, that individual is not wise concerning all things.

4. MEN WHO HAD THIS GIFT OF REVELATION

Who in the Bible possessed this gift? All the prophets of the Bible were endowed with this spiritual gift, in that they were seers of the future. They made known God's wisdom of what would come to pass.

A. God revealed to Noah the coming of the flood.

Genesis 6:12-13, *And God looked upon the earth, and, behold, it was corrupt; for all flesh had corrupted his way upon the earth.*

v. 13, *And God said unto Noah, The end of all flesh is come before me; for the earth is filled with violence through them; and, behold, I will destroy them with the earth.*

For over one hundred years before God actually did it, Noah knew that God would destroy the earth. This is the gift of the word of God's wisdom.

B. When Daniel saw the empires leap into existence and perform on the stage of human history before they were born, and named their very nature, it was the gift of the word of wisdom in operation (Daniel 7:2-28). It is said that this chapter, in its matter as well as its position in the central part of the book, is to the book of Daniel what the eighth chapter of Romans is to that epistle. Next to the fifty-third chapter of Isaiah and perhaps the ninth chapter also, we have here the most precious and prominent portion of the sure word of prophecy concerning the coming of the Messiah. The chapter is worthy of the most careful prayer and study. It is referred to directly or indirectly by Christ and His apostles perhaps more than other portions of the Old Testament of similar extent. It appears to have been regarded by the Old Testament saints, in the centuries preceding the Messiah's first advent, as pre-eminently the "word of prophecy." (Holiletic Commentary, adapted.)

C. The prophet Ezekiel dramatically foretold the future. Some passages such as Ezekiel 38, 39 and 40 have not yet come to pass. This shows how God reveals the future.

D. David revealed through his Psalms how the Messiah would come and how He would die. This was a revelation of the future (Psalm 2 and Psalm 22).

E. Joel prophesied that in the last days God's Spirit would be poured out upon all flesh. He was revealing the future which is the word of God's wisdom.

Joel 2:28, *And it shall come to pass afterward, that I will pour out my spirit upon all flesh; and your sons and your daughters shall prophesy, your old men shall dream dreams, your young men shall see visions.*

F. In Isaiah 53, the great prophet described the very nature of the Messiah. This was the word of God's wisdom functioning.

5. THE WORD OF WISDOM IN THE NEW TESTAMENT

The New Testament is replete with instances of the gift of the word of wisdom.

A. Foremost among those demonstrating the word of wisdom in the New Testament was the Lord Jesus. In Matthew 24, Mark 13 and Luke 21, Christ foretold the destruction of the temple which came a few years later, the signs which would accompany His return to earth for His church, and the end of the world. Many of these things are coming to pass in our generation. Some of them are yet to come to pass.

B. The Apostle Paul in I Thessalonians, I Timothy and other epistles, revealed things that would come to pass in the last days. This was the word of wisdom.

C. The Apostle Peter was very emphatic about signs that would come to pass before the Lord Jesus returned. This was the functioning of the word of wisdom.

D. The gift functioned for the Apostle Paul when it looked as if he would die. The Lord spoke to him the word of wisdom in Acts 23:11, *Be of good cheer, Paul: for as thou hast testified of me in Jerusalem, so must thou bear witness also at Rome.*

Paul had no way of knowing he would ever speak for God in Rome, but God revealed the future for his life.

6. THE WORD OF WISDOM MANIFESTED IN VARIOUS WAYS

The Holy Spirit can convey the word of wisdom in many ways.

A. To Joseph it was the interpreting of a dream of the future (Genesis 41).

B To Daniel it was a vision by night (Daniel 7).

C. Ezekiel was caught away in the Spirit for a revelation (Ezekiel 37).

D. The Apostle John was in the Spirit on the Lord's Day and the total book of Revelation flashed before him (Revelation 1:10).

This reveals that God has no set way of dealing with the problems of this world. He unveils the hidden mysteries of God and the wisdom of God, to execute His counsels in the way He sees best at that time.

7. A PERSONAL FUNCTION OF THE WORD OF WISDOM

A number of years ago in a simple wooden building in Tennessee, God showed me a vision that I was called to minister to the entire world. I saw the millions of the world marching past me into eternity. At the same time in London, England, God communicated a message to Rev. Howard Carter saying that he must travel the world to minister. God told him that He had prepared a companion for him who lived in a distant place. He would be a stranger when he came, and would make himself known by saying certain words. Reverend Carter was so impressed with this message from God that he wrote it down and disclosed it to his teaching staff and students in his Bible school in London.

Less than three years later, not knowing that God had spoken to Reverend Carter, I approached him at a camp meeting in Eureka Springs, Arkansas, and God fulfilled completely the words spoken to him in London, England. In his hotel room, Reverend Carter, Reverend Stanley Fordsham and I lifted up our hearts and thanked God that He could so speak in these days. That moment began one of the most remarkable friendships in our time as an Englishman and an American traveled throughout the world to minister and bless multitudes of people.

8. THE WORD OF WISDOM AND THE GIFT OF PROPHECY

A clear distinction must be formed in our minds regarding the simple inspirational gift of prophecy in the New Testament and the word of wisdom. I Corinthians 14:3 gives the full measure of the blessings of prophecy. There is no revelation associated with it. Any person who speaks in church and foretells the future has left the simplest and least of the gifts and has moved into the greatest and foremost.

The prophet of the Old Testament or the New Testament is a seer who sees the future and possesses the gift of the word of God's wisdom.

9. WE MUST COVET THIS GIFT

Most cults are born because the church does not utilize the gifts of God. For example, if the total church had prayed for the sick, Christian Science would have no place in the world.

If the church moved into the spiritual gifts of revelation, such as the word of wisdom, the word of knowledge and the discerning of spirits, there would be no need for fortune tellers, crystal ball gazers, Ouija boards, tea-leaf interpreters and all the paraphernalia which the devil uses to deceive the people of our generation.

The world is now engulfed in the greatest wave of black magic and witchcraft the world has ever known. One reason is that the church is not operating in the gifts of the Spirit. These gifts are the weapons of our warfare. If they were in operation, they would completely stop the devil's counterfeits.

Therefore, I challenge you to seek God for these major gifts of the Holy Spirit.

I Corinthians 12:31, *But covet earnestly the best gifts. . .*

I Corinthians 14:1, *. . .desire spiritual gifts. . .*

WORLD HARVEST SCHOOL OF CONTINUOUS LEARNING

STUDY: THE GIFTS AND MINISTRIES OF THE HOLY SPIRIT

LESSON 15

THE WORD OF KNOWLEDGE

INTRODUCTION:

The second gift in the category of revelation gifts is the gift of the word of knowledge. Knowledge is a fact. Knowledge deals with things as they now exist. Therefore, the gift of the word of knowledge is when God reveals to one of His servants something which now exists or did exist on the earth.

This would be something you could not know naturally. It would be something your eyes had not seen and your ears had not heard. Normally, it would have to do with the meeting of an emergency.

READING:

I Corinthians 12:8, *. . .to another the word of knowledge by the same spirit.*

1. **GOD IS OMNISCIENT**

   He knows all. He has all knowledge. God knows of every person and every place.

2. **A WORD OF KNOWLEDGE TO ELIJAH**

   I Kings 19:14, 18, *And he said, I have been very jealous for the LORD God of hosts: because the children of Israel have forsaken thy covenant, thrown down thine altars, and slain thy prophets with the sword; and I, even I only, am left; and they seek my life, to take it away.*

   v. 18, *Yet I have left me with seven thousand in Israel, all the knees which have not bowed unto Baal, and every mouth which hath not kissed him.*

3. **ELISHA AND GEHAZI**

II Kings 5:20, 27, *But, Gehazi, the servant of Elisha the man of God, said, Behold, my master hath spared Naaman this Syrian, in not receiving at his hands that which he brought: but, as the LORD liveth, I will run after him, and take somewhat of him.*

v. 27, *The leprosy therefore of Naaman shall cleave unto thee, and unto thy seed for ever. And he went out from his presence a leper as white as snow.*

He pursued Naaman and took silver and raiment. Elisha knew it by the Spirit.

4. **SAMUEL AND SAUL**

When Saul, a Benjamite, was called to be a king, he hid himself; however, the prophet knew where he was.

I Samuel 10:22, *Therefore they inquired of the LORD further, if the man should yet come thither. And the LORD answered, Behold, he hath hid himself among the stuff.*

5. **ELISHA KNEW THE ENEMY'S WAR PLANS**

In the Old Testament, the prophet Elisha used this gift in a remarkable way. In II Kings 6, he revealed the alien armies of Syria coming against the king of Israel. While sitting in his own house, he told the king how the armies would attack and how he could confront them. The Syrian king accused some of his intimates of treachery, but they assured him it was only the prophet of God.

6. **JESUS OPERATED IN THE WORD OF KNOWLEDGE**

A. In the New Testament, the Lord Jesus exercised this gift with great authority. For example, in John 1:47-50 when He saw Nathaniel He said, . . .*Behold an Israelite indeed, in whom is no guile!. . .Whence knowest thou me? Jesus answered and said unto him, Before that Philip called thee, when thou wast under the fig tree, I saw thee.*

Here, supernaturally, the Lord Jesus Christ saw this man the day before sitting under a fig tree. This was the word of God's knowledge.

B. In John 4:18, Jesus tells the Samaritan woman about herself. *For thou hast had five husbands; and he whom thou now hast is not thy husband: in that saidst thou truly.*

7. THE ACTS OF THE APOSTLES DESCRIBES THIS GIFT IN THE EARLY CHURCH

In Acts 10:19-21, Peter knew that the three messengers from Cornelius were on their way and would inquire for him at the gate of the house of Simon the Tanner. He greeted them with the words, *Behold, I am he whom ye seek.* This is a communication of God's knowledge.

8. WOMAN IN TULSA, OKLAHOMA

A Christian lady was told by God that her son and daughter were going fishing. She was told at which lake they were fishing. She was told that the son, his wife and two children were drowned. She even knew the place where they were drowned. When she called the fire and police departments, they hesitated to go to the site because of the way in which she received her knowledge of tragedy. Through her persistence they did go and found exactly what she had told them.

9. REVEREND HOWARD CARTER OF LONDON

After I had met Reverend Howard Carter in Eureka Springs, Arkansas, and we had agreed to travel together, he traveled to the west coast and I traveled south to take my sister home. It took me three months to sell my car, receive my passport from Washington and get ready for the world mission. During this time, I did not know where Reverend Carter was. I was told by some that he was in Japan, and by others that he was in China, and by others that he was in Indonesia. Not knowing in what part of the Orient he was, I purchased a ticket to Australia and decided to look for him from the bottom of the world to the top in Asia.

After three weeks at sea, my ship pulled into Wellington, New Zealand. Rev. Carter had been in a ministers' conference at a retreat. While praying, he asked the Lord where I was. The Lord replied, "He is at this time on a ship coming into Wellington Harbor. Tomorrow he will come to a certain pastor's home. Send him a message there."

The pastor from the church in Wellington was in the same conference. Reverend Carter said, "Tomorrow a young American will come to your home. Will you be so kind as to go and give him my card and tell him I will join him in Australia?" The minister asked, "But where did you get this information, seeing we have no telephone at this place?" Reverend Carter responded, "The Lord just spoke to me about it." The pastor actually went back to Wellington unbelieving.

The next morning after my ship docked, not knowing any of this had transpired, I went into the city and looked for this church. After three hours I found it and knocked at the door. The pastor opened the door and I said, "Sir, you do not know me, I am Lester Sumrall from America." The pastor stopped me and turned pale saying, "Yes, I know you. You are looking for Reverend Carter and I have a messsage from him to you."

This is the word of knowledge from God. God, knowing where I was, told Reverend Carter in order that we could labor together throughout the world.

10. THE PURPOSE OF THIS GIFT TODAY

Any time God conveys information supernaturally which has to do with that which is now in existence, it is the word of God's knowledge in operation. This gift could resolve many problems in churches. It could even resolve many national problems if the leaders of the nation had confidence and faith in God.

WORLD HARVEST SCHOOL OF CONTINUOUS LEARNING

STUDY: THE GIFTS AND MINISTRIES OF THE HOLY SPIRIT

LESSON 16

THE DISCERNING OF SPIRITS

INTRODUCTION:

The divine purpose and ministry of this gift is to discern the spirit that motivates a person, whether it be a good spirit from God or an evil spirit of the devil.

READING:

I Corinthians 12:10, . . .*to another discerning of spirits. . .*

1. **THERE ARE THREE AREAS OF OPERATION**

    A. Divine

    B. Demonic

    C. Human

2. **NOT DISCERNING OF DEVILS**

    Primarily, I must state emphatically this gift is not just the discerning of devils. It is not a *clash* of *human personalities.* It is not when a husband becomes angry with his wife and says she has a devil. It is by no means the gift of *suspicion* to try to see what spirit is in the people we meet.

    It certainly is not a study in psychoanalysis and it is not the projection of ESP (extra-sensory perception), which is a function of the human mind. The mind is a part of the soul and functions from the Spirit.

3. **INSIGHT INTO THE SPIRIT**

    This divine gift is the ability to see the presence or activity of a spirit whether good or bad. This revelation comes to the church through the Holy Spirit. The discerning of spirits gives the members of the Body of Christ an insight into the spirit world where their five senses of feeling, hearing, seeing, smelling and tasting cannot enter.

The telescope can reveal the movements of stars in space. The microscope can bring to light the intricate mysteries of microscopic life. In the realm of human affairs, the gift of the discerning of spirits can penetrate to the soul and spirit of a person.

4. DISCERNMENT AND THE LAST DAYS

Discerning of spirits is therefore a gift which enables one to appraise motives. More than this, it gives a believer power to see what others do not see. As Howard Carter pointed out, "The discerning of spirits is a gift of the Holy Spirit by which the possessor is enabled to see into the spirit world. By this insight he can discern the similitude of God, the risen Christ, the Holy Spirit, cherubim, seraphim, archangels or the host of angels, or Satan and his legions."

The discerning of spirits can bring great inspiration to the church. It can produce a sense of security against false doctrines, lies, etc., and enable the church to choose the proper men and women for their ministries.

5. WHAT REVELATION IS NOT

These three gifts, (the word of wisdom, the word of knowledge and the discerning of spirits) make up the gifts of revelation wherein God reveals something by His Spirit to the church.

A. It is not the reading of thoughts.

B. It is not metaphorical.

C. It is not extrasensory perception (e.s.p.).

6. PETER HAD DISCERNMENT

An example of the use of this gift is found in Acts 8:18. Simon the sorcerer looked on with wonder as Peter and John laid their hands on people and they would receive the Holy Ghost. He thought in his heart, "If only I had such power, it would make me a big man among people. Every man has his price. I will persuade these men to sell this power to me." So he offered the apostles money.

In Acts 8:20-23 we are shown Peter's response to this: *But Peter said unto him, Thy money perish with thee, because thou hast thought that the gift of God may be purchased with money. Thou hast neither part nor lot in this matter: for thy heart is not right in the sight of God. Repent therefore of this thy wickedness, and pray*

God, if perhaps the thought of thine heart may be forgiven thee. For I perceive that thou art in the gall of bitterness, and in the bond of iniquity.

7. PAUL DISCERNS A SORCERER

Another example is found in Acts 13:9-10. Here Paul discerns the evil tendencies of Elymas, the sorcerer.

Acts 13:9-10, *Then Saul, (who also is called Paul,) filled with the Holy Ghost, set his eyes on him,*

v. 10, *And said, O full of all subtilty and all mischief, thou child of the devil, thou enemy of all righteousness, wilt thou not cease to pervert the right ways of the Lord?*

8. THE HARLOT DISCERNED IN TENNESSEE

A number of years ago, I was present in a meeting where a strange woman came into the service. She stood to her feet and said, "God has told me to conduct a special revival campaign in this church and no one is to resist me because I am God's servant and the revival must begin tonight."

The people were dumbfounded. A strange feeling swept over them. There was a moment of murmuring, then quietness. An old godly lady to one side of the auditorium had sat all this time with bowed head. Finally she stood up, and with her face raised toward heaven said, "You are a harlot. You are from St. Louis, Missouri. You are in this city living with a man to whom you are not married. You have boasted that you could deceive this church, preach to them and collect an offering and they would never know you are a harlot. If you do not repent, you will die before you leave this building."

God's power fell heavily on the church and everyone went to their knees in prayer. When we lifted our heads the strange woman was gone, never to put in an appearance again. This was an operation of the discerning of spirits.

Some churches today would not want this gift in operation because sometimes pastors are living in sin, sometimes deacons are living in sin, sometimes musicians and singers are living in sin, and if this gift were in evidence it would be too revealing.

WORLD HARVEST SCHOOL OF CONTINUOUS LEARNING

STUDY: THE GIFTS AND MINISTRIES OF THE HOLY SPIRIT

LESSON 17

THE NINE MINISTRIES OF
THE HOLY SPIRIT TO THE CHURCH
PART 1

INTRODUCTION:

There are nine ministries to the church of Jesus Christ by the Holy Spirit. They are found in I Corinthians 12:28 and Ephesians 4:41.

1. Apostles	**4.** Evangelists	**7.** Deacons
2. Prophets	**5.** Teachers	**8.** Helps
3. Pastors	**6.** Elders or Bishops	**9.** Governments

READING:

Ephesians 4:11, *And he gave some, apostles; and some, prophets; and some, evangelists; and some, pastors and teachers.*

I Corinthians 12:28, *And God hath set some in the church, first apostles, secondarily prophets, thirdly teachers, after that miracles, then gifts of healings, helps, governments, diversities of tongues.*

1. **THESE ARE MEN AND WOMEN GIVEN TO THE CHURCH TO MINISTER**

   A. The apostle is the key to all the ministries and has the ability to perform all the ministries. This is the reason he is first. Any person who has an apostolic ministry can go and raise up a church as the founder. He can remain and pastor that church as a shepherd. He has the ability to teach the people. He is a combination of all the church ministries.

   The apostle knows how to set deacons and elders and helps and governments in the church body so the church might function properly.

B. There are also combinations of ministries.

1) For example, Stephen was chosen to be a deacon and he became a mighty teacher of the word.

Acts 6:5, *And the saying pleased the whole multitude: and they chose Stephen, a man full of faith and of the Holy Ghost, and Philip, and Prochorus, and Nicanor, and Timon, and Parmenas, and Nicolas a proselyte of Antioch.*

Acts 6:8, *And Stephen, full of faith and power, did great wonders and miracles among the people.*

Acts 6:9-10, *Then there arose certain of the synagogue, which is called the synagogue of the Libertines, and Cyrenians, and Alexandrians, and of them of Cilicia and of Asia, disputing with Stephen.*

v. 10, *And they were not able to resist the wisdom and the spirit by which he spake.*

2) Philip was chosen to be a deacon and he became a great evangelist who moved an entire city.

Acts 6:5-6, *And the saying pleased the whole multitude: and they chose Stephen, a man full of faith and of the Holy Ghost, and Philip, and Prochorus, and Nicanor, and Timon, and Parmenas, and Nicolas a proselyte of Antioch:*

v. 6, *Whom they set before the apostles: and when they had prayed, they laid their hands on them.*

Acts 8:5-8, *Then Philip went down to the city of Samaria, and preached Christ unto them.*

v. 6, *And the people with one accord gave heed unto those things which Philip spake, hearing and seeing the miracles which he did.*

v. 7, *For unclean spirits, crying with loud voice, came out of many that were possessed with them: and many taken with palsies, and that were lame, were healed.*

v. 8. *And there was great joy in that city.*

3) These are combination ministries. There are men who are teachers and yet pastors. They do both equally well. Some are evangelists and pastors and can do both equally well.

2. APOSTLES

A. There are several translations of the Greek word referring to apostles. *APOSTOLOS*—it means a delegate, one sent with full powers of attorney to act for another. It is found 81 times in the New Testament.

   1) It is translated "messenger" two times.

      II Corinthians 8:23, *Whether any do inquire of Titus, he is my partner and fellow-helper concerning you: or our brethren be inquired of, they are the messengers of the churches, and the glory of Christ.*

      Philippians 2:25, *Yet I supposed it necessary to send to you Epaphroditus, my brother, and companion in labour, and fellowsoldier, but your messenger, and he that ministered to my wants.*

   2) It is translated as "apostles" 78 times.

   3) It is translated "he that is sent" one time.

      John 13:16, *Verily, verily, I say unto you, The servant is not greater than his lord; neither he that is sent greater than he that sent him.*

B. There are 24 apostles in the New Testament.

   1) JESUS CHRIST: Hebrews 3:1, *Wherefore, holy brethren, partakers of the heavenly calling, consider the Apostle and High Priest of our profession, Christ Jesus.*

   2) PAUL: Galatians 1:1, *Paul, an apostle, (not of men, neither by man, but by Jesus Christ, and God the Father, who raised him from the dead;).*

      Galatians 2:8, *(For he that wrought effectually in Peter to the apostleship of the circumcision, the same was mighty in me toward the Gentiles:).*

   3) SIMON PETER: Matthew 10:2, *Now the names of the twelve apostles are these; The first, Simon, who is called Peter. . .*

   4) ANDREW: Matthew 10:2, *Now the names of the twelve apostles are these; The first, Simon who is called Peter, and Andrew his brother. . .*

   5) JAMES, SON OF ZEBEDEE: Matthew 10:2, *Now the names of the twelve apostles are these;. . .James, the son of Zebedee. . .*

   6) JOHN: Matthew 10:2, *Now the names of the twelve apostles are these;. . .John his brother. . .*

65

7) PHILIP: Matthew 10:2, *Now the names of the twelve apostles are these;. . .Philip. . .*

8) BARTHOLOMEW: Matthew 10:2, *Now the names of the twelve apostles are these;. . .Bartholomew. . .*

9) JAMES, SON OF ALPHAEUS: Matthew 10:2-3, *Now the names of the twelve apostles are these. . .*

   v. 3, *. . .James the son of Alphaeus. . .*

10) JUDAS, BROTHER OF JAMES: Luke 6:16, *And Judas the brother of James. . .*

11) MATTHEW: Luke 6:13, 15, *And when it was day, he called unto him his disciples: and of them he chose twelve, whom also he named apostles. . .*

   v. 15, *. . .Matthew. . .*

12) THOMAS: Matthew 10:2-3, *Now the names of the twelve apostles are these. . .*

   v. 3, *. . .Thomas. . .*

13) SIMON ZELOTES: Luke 6:13, 15, *. . .he chose twelve, whom also he named apostles. . .*

   v. 15, *. . .Simon called Zelotes. . .*

14) JUDAS ISCARIOT: Matthew 10:2, 4, *Now the names of the twelve apostles are these;*

   v. 4, *. . .Judas Iscariot, who also betrayed him.*

15) MATTHIAS: Acts 1:26, *And they gave forth their lots; and the lot fell upon Matthias; and he was numbered with the eleven apostles.*

16) BARNABAS: I Corinthians 9:5-6, *Have we not power to lead about a sister, a wife, as well as other apostles, and as the brethren of the Lord, and Cephas?*

   v. 6, *Or I only and Barnabas, have not we power to forbear working?*

17) ANDRONICUS: Romans 16:7, *Salute Andronicus and Junia, my kinsmen, and my fellow prisoners, who are of note among the apostles, who also were in Christ before me.*

18) JUNIA: Romans 16:7, *Salute. . .Junia. . .who are of note among the apostles. . .*

19) APOLLOS: I Corinthians 4:6-9, *And these things, brethren, I have in a figure transferred to myself and to Apollos for your sakes; that ye might learn in us not to think of men above that which is written, that no one of you be puffed up for one against another.*

v. 7, *For who maketh thee to differ from another? and what hast thou that thou didst not receive? now if thou didst receive it, why dost thou glory, as if thou hadst not received it?*

v. 8, *Now ye are full, now ye are rich, ye have reigned as kings without us: and I would to God ye did reign, that we also might reign with you.*

v. 9, *For I think that God hath set forth us the apostles last, as it were appointed to death: for we are made a spectacle unto the world, and to angels, and to men.*

20) JAMES THE LORD'S BROTHER: Galatians 1:19, *But other of the apostles saw I none, save James the Lord's brother.*

James 1:1, *James, a servant of God and of the Lord Jesus Christ, to the twelve tribes which are scattered abroad, greeting.*

21) SILAS: I Thessalonians 1:1, *Paul, and Silvanus, and Timotheus, unto the church of the Thessalonians. . .*

I Thessalonians 2:6, *Nor of men sought we glory, neither of you, nor yet of others, when we might have been burdensome, as the apostles of Christ.*

22) TIMOTHY: Same as above.

23) TITUS: II Corinthians 8:23, *Whether any do inquire of Titus, he is my partner and fellow-helper concerning you: or our brethren be inquired of, they are the messengers of the churches, and the glory of Christ.*

24) EPAPHRODITUS: Philippians 2:25, *Yet I supposed it necessary to send to you Epaphroditus, my brother, and companion in labour, and fellowsoldier, but your messenger, and he that ministered to my wants.*

C. APOSTLES TODAY

None of the ministries of the church have been withdrawn. The delegates or sent ones are ministering to the church body. The position cannot be voted upon by men. It is a calling of God.

Romans 1:1, 5, *Paul, a servant of Jesus Christ, called to be an apostle, separated unto the gospel of God,*

v. 5, *By whom we have received grace and apostleship. . .*

SYLLABUS

WORLD HARVEST SCHOOL OF CONTINUOUS LEARNING

STUDY: THE GIFTS AND MINISTRIES OF THE HOLY SPIRIT

LESSON 18

**THE NINE MINISTRIES OF
THE HOLY SPIRIT TO THE CHURCH
PART 2**

INTRODUCTION:

We saw from our last lesson that there are nine God-given ministries to function in the Church. They are a ministry, a life, a power. Not a title. They are: apostles, prophets, evangelists, pastors, teachers, elders, deacons, helps and governments.

READING:

Ephesians 4:11, *And he gave some, apostles; and some, prophets; and some, evangelists; and some, pastors and teachers.*

I Corinthians 12:28, *And God hath set some in the church, first apostles, secondarily prophets, thirdly teachers, after that miracles, then gifts of healings, helps, governments, diversities of tongues.*

1. **THE OFFICE OF APOSTLESHIP IS THE HIGHEST MINISTRY IN THE CHURCH**

   The office of apostleship was designated to at least 24 persons in the New Testament and to thousands of persons during the present church age.

2. **THE SECOND DIGNITARY OF THE CHURCH MINISTRY IS THE OFFICE OF THE PROPHET**

   A. There is a difference between a prophet and the single gift of the inspiration prophecy.

I Corinthians 14:3, *But he that prophesieth speaketh unto men to edification, and exhortation, and comfort.*

B. In the Old Testament the position of a prophet was that of a divine guide to lead the people of Israel. The prophet was also called SEER. I Samuel 9:9, *(Beforetime in Israel, when a man went to inquire of God, thus he spake, Come, and let us go to the seer: for he that is now called a Prophet was beforetime called a Seer.)*

The Hebrew words are A-RA-AH or seeing, perceiving person or CHOZEH or beholder of visions. I Samuel 24:11, *Moreover, my father, see, yea, see the skirt of thy robe in my hand: for in that I cut off the skirt of thy robe, and killed thee not, know thou and see that there is neither evil nor transgression in mine hand, and I have not sinned against thee; yet thou huntest my soul to take it.*

3. THE BIBLE LISTS 78 PROPHETS AND PROPHETESSES

Some of these include:

A. Adam was probably the first one. Genesis 2:19, *And out of the ground the LORD God formed every beast of the field, and every fowl of the air; and brought them unto Adam to see what he would call them: and whatsoever Adam called every living creature, that was the name thereof.*

B. Enoch: Genesis 5:21, *And Enoch lived sixty and five years, and begat Methuselah.* Methuselah means "at his death judgment would come." Methuselah lived 964 years and the flood came.

Jude 14, 15, *And Enoch also, the seventh from Adam, prophesied of these, saying, Behold, the Lord cometh with ten thousands of his saints,*

v 15, *To execute judgment upon all, and to convince all that are ungodly among them of their ungodly deeds which they have ungodly committed, and of all their hard speeches which ungodly sinners have spoken against him.*

C. Noah: Genesis 6:8-9, *But Noah found grace in the eyes of the LORD.*

v. 9, *These are the generations of Noah: Noah was a just man and perfect in his generations, and Noah walked with God.*

I Peter 3:20-21, *Which sometime were disobedient, when once the longsuffering of God waited in the days of Noah, while the ark was a-preparing, wherein few, that is, eight souls were saved by water.*

v. 21, *The like figure whereunto even baptism doth also now save us (not the putting away of the filth of the flesh, but the answer of a good conscience toward God,) by the resurrection of Jesus Christ.*

He prophesied of a flood of waters.

D. Eber: Genesis 10:25, *And unto Eber were born two sons: the name of one was Peleg; for in his days was the earth divided; and his brother's name was Joktan.*

The naming of his son was a prophecy of the dividing of the lands. At his birth the father predicted the breakup of the earth.

E. Abraham: Genesis 24:6-7, *And Abraham said unto him, Beware thou that thou bring not my son thither again.*

v. 7, *The LORD God of heaven, which took me from my father's house, and from the land of my kindred, and which spake unto me, and that sware unto me, saying, Unto thy seed will I give this land; he shall send his angel before thee, and thou shalt take a wife unto my son from thence.*

F. Jacob: Genesis 49:1, *And Jacob called unto his sons, and said, Gather yourselves together, that I may tell you that which shall befall you in the last days.*

G. Joseph: Genesis 41:15-16, 25, *And Pharaoh said unto Joseph, I have dreamed a dream, and there is none that can interpret it: and I have heard say of thee, that thou canst understand a dream to interpret it.*

v. 16, *And Joseph answered Pharaoh, saying, It is not in me: God shall give Pharoah an answer of peace.*

v. 25, . . .*The dream of Pharaoh is one: God hath shewed Pharaoh what he is about to do.*

H. Moses wrote 475 verses of prophecy. Exodus 11:4-8, *And Moses said, Thus saith the LORD, About midnight will I go into the midst of Egypt:*

v. 5, *And all the firstborn in the land of Egypt shall die, from the firstborn of Pharaoh that sitteth upon his throne, even unto the firstborn of the maidservant that is behind the mill; and all the firstborn of beasts.*

v. 6, *And there shall be a great cry throughout all the land of Egypt, such as there was none like it, nor shall be like it any more.*

v. 7, *But against any of the children of Israel shall not a dog move his tongue, against man or beast: that ye may know how that the LORD doth put a difference between the Egyptians and Israel.*

v. 8, *And all these thy servants shall come down unto me, and bow down themselves unto me, saying, Get thee out, and all the people that follow thee: and after that I will go out. And he went out from Pharaoh in a great anger.* . . .Fulfilled in Exodus 12:29-51.

I. Elijah: I Kings 18:41, *And Elijah said unto Ahab, Get thee up, eat and drink; for there is a sound of abundance of rain.* Fulfilled in I Kings 18:45.

J. Isaiah: Isaiah 7:14-16, *Therefore the Lord himself shall give you a sign; Behold, a virgin shall conceive, and bear a son, and shall call his name Immanuel.*

v. 15, *Butter and honey shall he eat, that he may know to refuse the evil, and choose the good.*

v. 16, *For before the child shall know to refuse the evil, and choose the good, the land that thou abhorrest shall be forsaken of both her kings.* Fulfilled in Matthew 1:18.

K. David wrote 385 verses of prophecy. Psalm 22:18, *They part my garments among them, and cast lots upon my vesture.* Fulfilled in Matthew 27:35.

L. Jeremiah wrote 985 verses of prophecy. Jeremiah 8:11, *For they have healed the hurt of the daughter of my people slightly, saying, Peace, peace; when there is no peace.* Fulfilled in I Thessalonians 5:3.

4. THERE WERE ALSO GROUPS OF PROPHETS

A. The 70 elders of Israel.

Numbers 11:25, *And the LORD came down in a cloud, and spake unto him, and took of the spirit that was upon him, and gave it unto the seventy elders: and it came to pass, that, when the spirit rested upon them, they prophesied, and did not cease.*

B. The schools of the prophets.

I Samuel 10:5-10, *After that thou shalt come to the hill of God, where is the garrison of the Philistines: and it shall come to pass, when thou art come thither to the city, that thou shalt meet a company of prophets coming down from the high place with a psaltery, and a tabret, and a pipe, and a harp, before them; and they shall prophesy:*

v. 6, *And the spirit of the LORD will come upon thee, and thou shalt prophesy with them, and shalt be turned into another man.*

v. 7, *And let it be, when these signs are come unto thee, that thou do as occasion serve thee; for God is with thee.*

v. 8, *And thou shalt go down before me to Gilgal; and, behold, I will come down unto thee, to offer burnt offerings, and to sacrifice sacrifices of peace offerings: seven days shalt thou tarry, till I come to thee, and shew thee what thou shalt do.*

v. 9, *And it was so, that when he had turned his back to go from Samuel, God gave him another heart: and all those signs came to pass that day.*

v. 10, *And when they came thither to the hill, behold, a company of prophets met him; and the spirit of God came upon him, and he prophesied among them.*

C. The sons of the prophets.

II Kings 2:3, *And the sons of the prophets that were at Beth-el came forth to Elisha, and said unto him, Knowest thou that the LORD will take away thy master from thy head today? And he said, Yea, I know it; hold ye your peace.*

5. THERE WERE 16 OLD TESTAMENT WRITING PROPHETS

These are found in the Bible from Isaiah to Malachi.

6. THERE WERE FOUR NEW TESTAMENT WRITING PROPHETS

A. Peter: Acts 2:16, *But this is that which was spoken by the prophet Joel.*

II Peter 3:3-7, *Knowing this first, that there shall come in the last days scoffers, walking after their own lusts.*

v. 4, *And saying, Where is the promise of his coming? for since the fathers fell asleep, all things continue as they were from the beginning of the creation.*

v. 5, *For this they willingly are ignorant of, that by the word of God the heavens were of old, and the earth standing out of the water and in the water:*

v. 6, *Whereby the world that then was, being overflowed with water, perished:*

v. 7, *But the heavens and the earth, which are now, by the same word are kept in store, reserved unto fire against the day of judgment and perdition of ungodly men.*

B. Paul: Acts 17:31, *Because he hath appointed a day, in the which he will judge the world in righteousness by that man whom he hath ordained; whereof he hath given assurance unto all men, in that he hath raised him from the dead.*

C.   James: James 5:1-8,   *Go to now, ye rich men, weep and howl for your miseries that shall come upon you.*

v. 2,   *Your riches are corrupted, and your garments are motheaten.*

v. 3,   *Your gold and silver is cankered; and the rust of them shall be a witness against you, and shall eat your flesh as it were fire. Ye have heaped treasure together for the last days.*

v. 4,   *Behold, the hire of the labourers who have reaped down your fields, which is of you kept back by fraud, crieth: and the cries of them which have reaped are entered into the ears of the Lord of sabaoth.*

v. 5,   *Ye have lived in pleasure on the earth, and been wanton; ye have nourished your hearts, as in a day of slaughter.*

v. 6,   *Ye have condemned and killed the just; and he doth not resist you.*

v. 7,   *Be patient therefore, brethren, unto the coming of the Lord. Behold, the husbandman waiteth for the precious fruit of the earth, and hath long patience for it, until he receive the early and latter rain.*

v. 8,   *Be ye also patient; stablish your hearts: for the coming of the Lord draweth nigh.*

D.   John: I John 2:17-18,   *And the world passeth away, and the lust thereof: but he that doeth the will of God abideth for ever.*

v. 18,   *Little children, it is the last time: and as ye have heard that antichrist shall come, even now are there many antichrists; whereby we know that it is the last time.*

Revelation 1:1,   *The Revelation of Jesus Christ, which God gave unto him, to shew unto his servants things which must shortly come to pass; and he sent and signified it by his angel unto his servant John.*

7.   THE NEW TESTAMENT ALSO INCLUDES SEVERAL PROPHETS.

A.   John The Baptist was the first New Testament prophet. Matthew 3:11-12,   *I indeed baptize you with water unto repentance: but he that cometh after me is mightier than I, whose shoes I am not worthy to bear: he shall baptize you with the Holy Ghost, and with fire.*

v. 12,   *Whose fan is in his hand, and he will thoroughly purge his floor, and gather his wheat into the garner; but he will burn up the chaff with unquenchable fire.*

John 1:29-34,   *The next day John seeth Jesus coming unto him, and saith, Behold the Lamb of God, which taketh away the sin of the world.*

v. 30, *This is he of whom I said, After me cometh a man which is preferred before me: for he was before me.*

v. 31, *And I knew him not: but that he should be made manifest to Israel, therefore am I come baptizing with water.*

v. 32, *And John bare record, saying, I saw the Spirit descending from heaven like a dove, and it abode upon him.*

v. 33, *And I knew him not: but he that sent me to baptize with water, the same said unto me, Upon whom thou shalt see the Spirit descending, and remaining on him, the same is he which baptizeth with the Holy Ghost.*

v. 34, *And I saw, and bare record that this is the Son of God.*

B. Zacharias: Luke 1:67-79, *And his father Zacharias was filled with the Holy Ghost, and prophesied, saying,*
v. 68, *Blessed be the Lord God of Israel; for he hath visited and redeemed his people,*

v. 69, *And hath raised up an horn of salvation for us in the house of his servant David;*

v. 70, *As he spake by the mouth of his holy prophets, which have been since the world began:*

v. 71, *That we should be saved from our enemies, and from the hand of all that hate us;*

v. 72, *To perform the mercy promised to our fathers, and to remember his holy covenant;*

v. 73, *The oath which he sware to our father Abraham,*

v. 74, *That he would grant unto us, that we being delivered out of the hand of our enemies might serve him without fear,*

v. 75, *In holiness and righteousness before him, all the days of our life.*

v. 76, *And thou, child, shalt be called the prophet of the Highest: for thou shalt go before the face of the Lord to prepare his ways;*

v. 77, *To give knowledge of salvation unto his people by the remission of their sins,*

v. 78, *Through the tender mercy of our God; whereby the dayspring from on high hath visited us,*

v. 79, *To give light to them that sit in darkness and in the shadow of death, to guide our feet into the way of peace.*

C. Simeon: Luke 1:25-35, *Thus hath the Lord dealt with me in the days wherein he looked on me, to take away my reproach among men.*

v. 26, *And in the sixth month the angel Gabriel was sent from God unto a city of Galilee, named Nazareth,*

v. 27, *To a virgin espoused to a man whose name was Joseph, of the house of David; and the virgin's name was Mary.*

v. 28, *And the angel came in unto her, and said, Hail, thou that art highly favoured, the Lord is with thee: blessed art thou among women.*

v. 29, *And when she saw him, she was troubled at his saying, and cast in her mind what manner of salutation this should be.*

v. 30, *And the angel said unto her, Fear not, Mary: for thou hast found favour with God.*

v. 31, *And, behold, thou shalt conceive in thy womb, and bring forth a son, and shalt call his name JESUS.*

v. 32, *He shall be great, and shall be called the Son of the Highest: and the Lord God shall give unto him the throne of his father David:*

v. 33, *And he shall reign over the house of Jacob for ever; and of his kingdom there shall be no end.*

v. 34, *Then said Mary unto the angel, How shall this be, seeing I know not a man?*

v. 35, *And the angel answered and said unto her, The Holy Ghost shall come upon thee: and the power of the Highest shall overshadow thee: therefore also that holy thing which shall be born of thee shall be called the Son of God.*

D. Agabus: Acts 11:28, *And there stood up one of them named Agabus, and signified by the Spirit that there should be great dearth throughout all the world: which came to pass in the days of Claudius Cæsar.*

Acts 21:10-11, *And as we tarried there many days, there came down from Judæa a certain prophet, named Agabus.*

v. 11, *And when he was come unto us, he took Paul's girdle, and bound his own hands and feet, and said, Thus saith the Holy Ghost, So shall the Jews at Jerusalem bind the man that owneth this girdle, and shall deliver him into the hands of the Gentiles.*

E. Ananias: Acts 9:15-16, *But the Lord said unto him, Go thy way: for he is a chosen vessel unto me, to bear my name before the Gentiles, and kings, and the children of Israel:*

v. 16,   *For I will shew him how great things he must suffer for my name's sake.*

F.   Barnabas, Simeon, Lucius and Manaen: Acts 13:1-2,   *Now there were in the church that was at Antioch certain prophets and teachers; as Barnabas, and Simeon that was called Niger, and Lucius of Cyrene, and Manaen, which had been brought up with Herod the tetrarch, and Saul.*

v. 2,   *As they ministered to the Lord, and fasted, the Holy Ghost said, Separate me Barnabas and Saul for the work whereunto I have called them.*

8.   PROPHETS SPOKE TO DIFFERENT GROUPS

A.   Individuals—Peter to Ananias and Saphira (Acts 5:3, 9).

B.   To a nation—Old Testament prophets to Israel (Hosea 9:1).

C.   To the world—Jeremiah 1:5,   *Before I formed thee in the belly, I knew thee; and before thou camest out of the womb I sanctified thee, and I ordained thee a prophet unto the nations.*

9.   FEMALE PROPHETS OF THE BIBLE

There have been a number of prophetesses in the scripture. God has used women in the most conventional and unconventional ways.

A.   Miriam: Exodus 15:20,   *And Miriam the prophetess, the sister of Aaron, took a timbrel in her hand; and all the women went out after her with timbrels and with dances.*

B.   Deborah: Judges 4:4,   *And Deborah, a prophetess, the wife of Lapidoth, she judged Israel at the time.*

C.   Huldah: II Kings 22:14,   *So Hilkiah the priest, and Ahikam, and Achbor, and Shaphan, and Asahiah, went unto Huldah the prophetess, the wife of Shallum the son of Tikvah, the son of Harhas, keeper of the wardrobe; (now she dwelt in Jerusalem in the college:) and they communed with her.*

D.   Noadiah: Nehemiah 6:14,   *My God, think thou upon Tobiah and Sanballat according to these their works, and on the prophetess Noadiah, and the rest of the prophets, that would have put me in fear.*

E.   Isaiah's wife: Isaiah 8:3,   *And I went unto the prophetess; and she conceived, and bare a son. Then said the LORD to me, Call his name Ma-her-shal-al-hash-baz.*

F.   Anna: Luke 2:36,   *And there was one Anna, a prophetess the daughter of Phanuel, of the tribe of Aser: she was of a great age, and had lived with an husband seven years from her virginity.*

10. MINISTRY OF THE NEW TESTAMENT PROPHET

A. John the Baptist—Heralded the presence of the Messiah.

B. Jesus—Prophesied of the coming of the Holy Spirit.

C. Matthew—Prophesied of end-time conditions.

D. Mark—Prophesied of the signs that shall follow them that believe.

E. John—Prophesied this same Jesus would return.

F. Ananias—Acts 9:15, *But the Lord said unto him, Go thy way: for he is a chosen vessel unto me, to bear my name before the Gentiles, and kings, and the children of Israel.*

G. Agabus—Acts 11:28, *And there stood up one of them named Agabus, and signified by the Spirit that there should be great dearth throughout all the world: which came to pass in the days of Claudius Cæsar.*

H. Barnabas—Simeon—Acts 13:1.

I. John—in the book of Revelation.

v. 16, *From whom the whole body fitly joined together and compacted by that which every joint supplieth, according to the effectual working in the measure of every part, maketh increase of the body unto the edifying of itself in love.*

These verses give us the ninefold purpose of the ministry.

a. "For the perfecting of the saints."

b. "For the work of the ministry."

c. "For the edifying of the body of Christ."

d. "Till we all come in the unity of the faith, and of the knowledge of the Son of God."

e. "Unto a perfect man."

f. "Unto the measure of the stature of the fulness of Christ."

g. "That we henceforth be no more children, tossed to and fro, and carried about with every wind of doctrine, by the sleight of men, and cunning craftiness, whereby they lie in wait to deceive."

h. "But speaking the truth in love, may grow up into him in all things, which is the head, even Christ."

i. "From whom the whole body fitly joined together and compacted by that which every joint supplieth, according to the effectual working in the measure of every part, maketh increase of the body unto the edifying of itself in love."

2. **THE GIFTS WERE GIVEN UNTO MEN**

"And he gave some, apostles; and some, prophets; and some, evangelists; and some, pastors and teachers" (Ephesians 4:11).

These gifts were given unto men. Christ gave these ministry gifts to the church. They are men called and anointed of God to stand in one of these five offices.

v. 16, *From whom the whole body fitly joined together and compacted by that which every joint supplieth, according to the effectual working in the measure of every part, maketh increase of the body unto the edifying of itself in love.*

1) The perfecting of the saints.
2) Work of the ministry.
3) Edifying of the body of Christ.
4) Till we all come in the unity of the faith.
5) To the knowledge of the Son of God.
6) Unto a perfect man.
7) Unto the measure of the stature of the fulness of Christ.

2. EVANGELISTS

A. Acts 21:8, *And the next day we that were of Paul's company departed, and came unto Cæsarea: and we entered into the house of Philip the evangelist, which was one of the seven; and abode with him.*

B. II Timothy 4:5, *But watch thou in all things, endure afflictions, do the work of an evangelist, make full proof of thy ministry.*

3. PASTORS

A. The Greek word *POIMEN* is used only once and translated as "pastor" (Ephesians 4:11).

B. The word "shepherd" is used 16 times in the New Testament.

Matthew 9:36, *But when he saw the multitudes, he was moved with compassion on them, because they fainted, and were scattered abroad, as sheep having no shepherd.*

C. The Hebrew word *RAAH* means to tend the flock and is translated "pastor" eight times.

Jeremiah 2:8, *The priests said not, Where is the LORD? and they that handle the law knew me not: the pastors also transgressed against me, and the prophets prophesied by Baal, and walked after things that do not profit.*

Jeremiah 3:15, *And I will give you pastors according to mine heart, which shall feed you with knowledge and understanding.*

D. "Shepherd" is used 63 times in the Old Testament.

4. TEACHERS

Acts 13:1-2, *Now there were in the church that was at Antioch certain prophets and* teachers; as Barnabas, and Simeon that was called Niger, and Lucius of Cyrene, and Manaen, which had been brought up with Herod the tetrarch, and Saul.

v. 2, As they ministered to the Lord, and fasted, the Holy Ghost said, Separate me Barnabas and Saul for the work whereunto I have called them.

5. ELDERS

A. I Timothy 3:1, This is a true saying, If a man desire the office of a bishop, he desireth a good work.

B. I Timothy 5:17-19, Let the elders that rule well be counted worthy of double honour, especially they who labour in the word and doctrine.

v. 18, For the scripture saith, Thou shalt not muzzle the ox that treadeth out the corn. And, The labourer is worthy of his reward.

v. 19, Against an elder receive not an accusation, but before two or three witnesses.

C. Acts 20:17, And from Miletus he sent to Ephesus, and called the elders of the church.

D. James 5:14, Is any sick among you? let him call for the elders of the church; and let them pray over him, anointing him with oil in the name of the Lord.

E. Acts 14:23, And when they had ordained them elders in every church, and had prayed with fasting, they commended them to the Lord, on whom they believed.

F. Titus 1:5-9, For this cause left I thee in Crete, that thou shouldest set in order the things that are wanting, and ordain elders in every city, as I had appointed thee:

v. 6, If any be blameless, the husband of one wife, having faithful children not accused of riot or unruly.

v. 7, For a bishop must be blameless, as the steward of God; not selfwilled, not soon angry, not given to wine, no striker, not given to filthy lucre;

v. 8, But a lover of hospitality, a lover of good men, sober, just, holy, temperate;

v. 9, Holding fast the faithful word as he hath been taught, that he may be able by sound doctrine both to exhort and to convince the gainsayers.

G. I Peter 5:1-4, The elders which are among you I exhort, who am also an elder, and a witness of the sufferings of Christ, and also a partaker of the glory that shall be revealed:

v. 2, Feed the flock of God which is among you, taking the oversight thereof, not by constraint, but willingly; not for filthy lucre, but of a ready mind;

v. 3,   *Neither as being lords over God's heritage, but being ensamples to the flock.*

v. 4,   *And when the chief Shepherd shall appear, ye shall receive a crown of glory that fadeth not away.*

6. DEACONS

A. The first deacons in the church were in Acts 6:1,   *And in those days, when the number of disciples was multiplied, there arose a murmuring of the Grecians against the Hebrews, because their widows were neglected in the daily ministration.*

B. I Timothy 3:8-13,   *Likewise must the deacons be grave, not double-tongued, not given to much wine, not greedy of filthy lucre;*

v. 9,   *Holding the mystery of the faith in a pure conscience.*

v. 10,   *And let these also first be proved; then let them use the office of a deacon, being found blameless.*

v. 11,   *Even so must their wives be grave, not slanderers, sober, faithful in all things.*

v. 12,   *Let the deacons be the husbands of one wife, ruling their children and their own houses well.*

v. 13,   *For they that have used the office of a deacon well purchase to themselves a good degree, and great boldness in the faith which is in Christ Jesus.*

7. HELPS

A. I Corinthians 12:28,   *And God hath set some in the church, first apostles, secondarily prophets, thirdly teachers, after that miracles, then gifts of healings, helps, governments, diversities of tongues.*

B. The New Testament is full of helps. The word "helps" in Acts 27:17 speaks of rope like cable that ships took along to wrap around it to hold it together during a storm.

C. Phebe who carried the book of Romans to Rome was a help.

Romans 16:1,   *I commend unto you Phebe our sister, which is a servant of the church which is at Cenchrea.*

D. Lydia who received Paul and gave him supper was a help.

Acts 16:14-15,   *And a certain woman named Lydia, a seller of purple, of the city of Thyatira, which worshipped God, heard us: whose heart the Lord opened, that she attended unto the things which were spoken of Paul.*

v. 15, *And when she was baptized, and her household, she besought us, saying, If ye have judged me to be faithful to the Lord, come into my house, and abide there. And she constrained us.*

E. Jesus said if you give a drink of water to a prophet, you receive a prophet's reward. That is a help.

Matthew 10:40-42, *He that receiveth you receiveth me, and he that receiveth me receiveth him that sent me.*

v. 41, *He that receiveth a prophet in the name of a prophet shall receive a prophet's reward; and he that receiveth a righteous man in the name of a righteous man shall receive a righteous man's reward.*

v. 42, *And whosoever shall give to drink unto one of these little ones a cup of cold water only in the name of a disciple, verily I say unto you, he shall in no wise lose his reward.*

F. Visitation of the sick is a help.

G. Office work is a help.

H. Television work is a help.

I. Giving of funds to support the work of God is a help.

J. Aaron and Hur who held up the arms of Moses were helps.

Exodus 17:12, *But Moses' hands were heavy; and they took a stone, and put it under him, and he sat thereon; and Aaron and Hur stayed up his hands, the one on the one side, and the other on the other side; and his hands were steady until the going down of the sun.*

8. GOVERNMENTS

A. I Corinthians 12:28, *And God hath set some in the church, first apostles, secondarily prophets, thirdly teachers, after that miracles, then gifts of healings, helps, governments, diversities of tongues.*

B. The Greek word *Kubemesis* means "to steer" or "to guide."

C. It has no reference to power and rule. Those who possess knowledge to steer the church and guide the church around its problems are the governments. This means that mature men and women under God's anointing are able to bless the church through spiritual government. These people could be deacons and elders yet they are serving here in a different role. They are functioning in the position of governments.

STUDY: THE GIFTS AND MINISTRIES OF THE HOLY SPIRIT

LESSON 20

THE DEVIL'S COUNTERFEITS OF THE NINE GIFTS

INTRODUCTION:

We understand that anything of inestimable value the devil will try to counterfeit. The devil has sought to counterfeit all the nine gifts of the Holy Spirit.

READING:

Revelation 13:14, *And deceiveth them that dwell on the earth by the means of those miracles which he had power to do in the sight of the beast; saying to them that dwell on the earth, that they should make an image to the beast, which had the wound by a sword, and did live.*

1. **THE WORD OF WISDOM**

   I Corinthians 12:8-10, *For to one is given by the Spirit the word of wisdom; to another the word of knowledge by the same Spirit;*

   v. 9, *To another faith by the same Spirit; to another the gifts of healing by the same Spirit;*

   v. 10, *To another the working of miracles; to another prophecy; to another discerning of spirits; to another divers kinds of tongues; to another the interpretation of tongues.*

   A. Witches seek to reveal the future.

   B. Soothsayers and magicians seek to know the unknown.

   C. God spoke through the Apostle Paul in II Corinthians 11:13-15, *For such are false apostles, deceitful workers, transforming themselves into the apostles of Christ.*

   v. 14, *And no marvel; for Satan himself is transformed into an angel of light.*

   v. 15, *Therefore it is no great thing if his ministers also be transformed as the ministers of righteousness; whose end shall be according to their works.*

83

2. THE WORD OF KNOWLEDGE

I Corinthians 12:8, . . .*to another the word of knowledge by the same Spirit.*

A. Palm reading is an attempt to know the present supernaturally.

B. Gold finding is trying to know where to look for treasure.

C. Fortunetelling is the devil's counterfeit.

3. THE DISCERNING OF SPIRITS

I Corinthians 12:10, . . .*to another discerning of spirits. . .*

The following are attempts at knowing spirits, but with the wrong source:

A. Mind reading

B. ESP

C. Gurus

D. Ouija Boards

4. GIFT OF FAITH

I Corinthians 12:9, . . .*To another faith by the same Spirit.* God does things for you supernaturally.

5. THE WORKING OF MIRACLES

I Corinthians 12:10, . . .*To another the working of miracles.*

A. The devil attempts to perform the supernatural through human means.

B. The witch doctor in Java could float in the air. This was a counterfeit of God's beautiful gift.

6. THE GIFTS OF HEALING

I Corinthians 12:9, . . .*to another the gifts of healing by the same Spirit.*

A. Witches seek to heal by potions, fetishes, and curses.

B. Cults claim to heal by curses.

7. THE GIFT OF PROPHECY

I Corinthians 12:10,. . .*to another prophecy.*

A. Some speak when God has not said anything. False prophets seek to deceive.

Acts 13:6-12, *And when they had gone through the isle unto Paphos, they found a certain sorcerer, a false prophet, a Jew, whose name was Bar-jesus:*

v. 7, *Which was with the deputy of the country, Sergius Paulus, a prudent man, who called for Barnabas and Saul, and desired to hear the word of God.*

v. 8, *But Elymas the sorcerer (for so is his name by interpretation) withstood them, seeking to turn away the deputy from the faith.*

v. 9, *Then Saul, (who also is called Paul,) filled with the Holy Ghost, set his eyes on him,*

v. 10, *And said, O full of all subtilty and all mischief, thou child of the devil, thou enemy of all righteousness, wilt thou not cease to pervert the right ways of the Lord?*

v. 11, *And now, behold, the hand of the Lord is upon thee, and thou shalt be blind, not seeing the sun for a season. And immediately there fell on him a mist and a darkness; and he went about seeking some to lead him by the hand.*

v. 12, *Then the deputy, when he saw what was done, believed, being astonished at the doctrine of the Lord.*

B. Revelation 16:13-14, *And I saw three unclean spirits like frogs come out of the mouth of the dragon, and out of the mouth of the beast, and out of the mouth of the false prophet.*

v. 14, *For they are the spirits of the devils, working miracles, which go forth unto the kings of the earth and of the whole world, to gather them to the battle of that great day of God Almighty.*

8. THE GIFT OF SPEAKING IN TONGUES

I Corinthians 12:10, *. . .to another the interpretation of tongues.*

I have heard false tongues coming forth from demon-possessed people.

9. THE INTERPRETATION OF TONGUES

I Corinthians 12:10, *. . .to another divers kinds of tongues.*

Devils seek to reveal mysteries and seek to interpret the unknown. These are deceptions.

10. THE ANTICHRIST WILL COUNTERFEIT THE GIFTS OF THE SPIRIT

A. The devil gave life to an image. The image of gold or silver spoke words from the devil.

Revelation 13:15, . . .*And he had power to give life unto the image of the beast, that the image of the beast should both speak, and cause that as many as would not worship the image of the beast should be killed.*

B. Miracles

Revelation 13:14, *And deceiveth them that dwell on the earth by the means of those miracles which he had power to do in the sight of the beast; saying to them that dwell on the earth, that they should make an image to the beast, which had the wound by a sword, and did live.*

C. Healing of deadly wound.

Revelation 13:11-12, *And I beheld another beast coming up out of the earth; and he had two horns like a lamb, and he spake as a dragon.*

v. 12, *And he exerciseth all the power of the first beast before him, and causeth the earth and them which dwell therein to worship the first beast, whose deadly wound was healed.*

D. Fire comes down from heaven in the sight of men.

Revelation 13:13, *And he doeth great wonders, so that he maketh fire come down from heaven on the earth in the sight of men.*

WORLD HARVEST SCHOOL OF CONTINUOUS LEARNING

STUDY: THE GIFTS AND MINISTRIES OF THE HOLY SPIRIT

LESSON 21

THE GIFT OF FAITH

INTRODUCTION:

We observe the gift of faith in operation when God, through the power of the Holy Spirit, performs supernatural exploits for a human when there is no human strength involved. In this gift God does something supernaturally for you.

READING:

I Corinthians 12:9, *To another faith by the same Spirit. . .*

1. **THE GIFTS ARE LIKE A CHAIN**

   We have now studied I Corinthians 12 about the divine unity of the gifts. There are diversities of gifts but the same Lord; these worketh that one and selfsame spirit. The gifts are closely associated, like links in a chain, that often makes definition very difficult. We will observe this closeness in the gifts of power now under consideration. The gifts are separate, yet they are one in the Holy Spirit, connected together like the links of a chain.

2. **MANY KINDS OF FAITH**

   Faith is like tea. Maybe the gift of faith is misunderstood with general faith in importance before the gifts of healing or working of miracles.

   We recognize many kinds of faith. Every person has a measure of faith. Each human has a natural faith. The faith the farmer has when he sows his seed, the faith a fisherman has when he casts his hook.

   There is also a saving faith. The thief on the cross had such faith; the Philippian jailer had such faith. We need faith to become converted and we need faith to walk with God, but the gift of faith is a special faith which achieves supernaturally what is impossible by human instruments. It is a sign gift from the Holy Spirit.

3. DANIEL HAD THE GIFT OF FAITH

When Daniel was placed in the den of lions he was immediately the master of the situation. He did not hurt the beasts. He did not ask God for power to tear them to pieces. Daniel simply radiated a force which caused the lions to lie down in perfect rest as Daniel slept among them. He personally did nothing, it was God who performed the amazing miracle.

4. THE THREE HEBREW CHILDREN DEMONSTRATED THE GIFT OF FAITH

When the three Hebrew children were placed in the fiery furnace, they did not fight the flames. They did not resist the flames. They did not put out the fire. God supernaturally preserved them.

5. GEORGE MUELLER OF BRISTOL, ENGLAND

Mr. George Mueller of Bristol, England, demonstrated the gift of faith with amazing results. Without any human effort to raise funds, such as letter writing, or lecturing, he fed thousands of orphans through the gift which God had given him to believe for the impossible. Many times he was tested, but everytime at the moment of need, the provision was present.

6. REVEREND HOWARD CARTER OF LONDON, ENGLAND

A. Reverend Howard Carter often demonstrated this gift of faith in his life and ministry. Once he purchased a church in London by faith. He simply committed himself to do it but had no funds. He was president of Hampstead Bible School and the faculty and students were greatly concerned because he had made the commitment possessing no funds. The time came for the final payment to be made and he did not have one cent. The students and teachers were greatly troubled and spent much time in prayer, but Brother Carter said, "God has assured me I will have this full payment on schedule."

The night before the final day of foreclosure on the property, the teachers and the students were worried and upset. They thought the next day would be the day of great embarrassment and the loss of the church. Reverend Carter on the other hand, was anything but ill-at-ease. He said, "We do not need money until tomorrow morning."

The last mail delivery in London was at 9:00 p.m. As Reverend Carter picked up the mail from the box at the Hampstead Bible School there was a large brown envelope. Whe he opened it, there in cash pounds was the total amount necessary to pay off the church. At breakfast the following morning he revealed the good news to the great relief of those who were concerned. There was no name or address of the donor.

B. Howard Carter and the reversal of gravitation—The gift of faith was used remarkably in the ministry of Howard Carter on one occasion during World War I. As a conscientious objector, Reverend Carter was placed in a work camp. His cell was small, uncomfortable and damp. Overhead water dripped on him incessantly, almost driving him mad. After suffering this for some time, he prayed and said in the Spirit, "I command you, water, to flow the other way." Reverend Carter testifies that immediately the water ceased to fall from that crack in the ceiling. It was dynamic faith in action.

7. THE GIFT OF FAITH IS UNLIMITED

The gift of faith has been manifested by many of God's people. It is evidenced when a supernatural event occurs with no human effort. Faith permits God to perform. This gift is unlimited because God is the source of its energy.

8. FAITH HAS TO DO WITH BEING "MORE THAN CONQUERORS"

The battle is won, but God wins it for you.

Romans 8:37, *Nay, in all these things we are more than conquerors through him that loved us.*

9. JESUS SPOKE TO THE FIG TREE

Matthew 21:19, *And when he saw a fig tree in the way, he came to it, and found nothing thereon, but leaves only, and said unto it, Let no fruit grow on thee henceforward for ever. And presently the fig tree withered away.*

The next day, Jesus didn't pay any attention to the fig tree. He had finished His work. His disciples wondered if it really happened and went over to have a look. The fig tree had died from the roots up, not from the leaves down.

We often ask why the Lord did this. That particular tree always had fruit before it had leaves. And when it had leaves but no fruit, it was a hypocrite. And Jesus said, "Because you are parading as having something you do not, you will die." This only reveals that Jesus never likes hypocrites.

10. JESUS AND THE STORM

Mark 4:37, *And there arose a great storm of wind, and the waves beat into the ship, so that it was now full.*

Luke 8:23, *But as they sailed he fell asleep: and there came down a storm of wind on the lake; and they were filled with water, and were in jeopardy.*

Jesus spoke one word. . .peace! The disciples were amazed and said, *What manner of man is this?* It was the force and the pungency of a gift called faith where no human strength of any nature is used. But God does it through His mighty power. The gift of faith is God doing something for you Himself, and you have nothing to do with it.

11. TWELVE LEGIONS OF ANGELS

A. Matthew 26:53, *Thinkest thou that I cannot now pray to my Father, and he shall presently give me more than twelve legions of angels?*

A legion is a minimum of 2,000! Jesus is talking about 24,000 plus! Faith is commanding the legions of heaven to perform on our behalf.

B. Acts 16:25, *And at midnight Paul and Silas prayed, and sang praises unto God: and the prisoners heard them.*

Paul and Silas had irons on and had been beaten with stripes. They could not help themselves because their hands and feet were in bondage. In a dirty dungeon, with blood running down their backs from the lashes of a whip, they began singing praises to God. The jail began to shake. Their bonds dropped off and the doors flew open. The jailer came in wanting to know what he could do to be saved.

12. THE GIFT OF FAITH CAN OPERATE IN THE AREA OF DIVINE PROTECTION

I Kings 17:3-6, *Get thee hence, and turn thee eastward, and hide thyself by the brook Cherith, that is before Jordan.*

v. 4, *And it shall be, that thou shalt drink of the brook; and I have commanded the ravens to feed thee there.*

v. 5, *So he went and did according unto the word of the LORD: for he went and dwelt by the brook Cherith, that is before Jordan.*

v. 6, *And the ravens brought him bread and flesh in the morning, and bread and flesh in the evening; and he drank of the brook.*

Elijah had to supernaturally believe.

13. MOSES THREW DOWN HIS ROD

Exodus 4:2-4, *And the LORD said unto him, What is that in thine hand? And he said, A rod.*

90

v. 3, *And he said, Cast it on the ground. And he cast it on the ground, and it became a serpent; and Moses fled from before it.*

v. 4, *And the LORD said unto Moses, Put forth thine hand, and take it by the tail. And he put forth his hand, and caught it, and it became a rod in his hand.*

Moses had faith it would happen.

14. ELISHA AND THE IRON AXE HEAD

II Kings 6:5-6, *But as one was felling a beam, the axe head fell into the water: and he cried, and said, Alas, master! for it was borrowed.*

v. 6, *And the man of God said, Where fell it? And he shewed him the place. And he cut down a stick, and cast it in thither; and the iron did swim.*

Elisha spoke, God did the rest.

SYLLABUS

WORLD HARVEST SCHOOL OF CONTINUOUS LEARNING

STUDY: THE GIFTS AND MINISTRIES OF THE HOLY SPIRIT

LESSON 22

THE GIFT OF WORKING OF MIRACLES

INTRODUCTION:

In the category of power, we now deal with the gift of working of miracles.

A happening is only a miracle as far as man is concerned. God, having all power, does not recognize miracles. What is a miracle to man is only an act with God. It is a miracle with man because he would not be able to perform this by his own natural strength.

The Greek words for "working of miracles" are *energemata dunameon.* From the first word, we derive our word *energy.* From the second word, we derive our word *dynamite.* The second word for miracles or *dunameon,* is the same word that is translated *power* in Acts 1:8. Thus we could say this is the gift of "energy of dynamite," or "explosion of almightiness."

The gift of the working of miracles means the supernatural intervention by God in the ordinary course of nature. In this gift, God works through a man or through some instrument.

READING:

I Corinthians 12:10, *To another the working of miracles. . .*

1. **THE DUMB ASS SPOKE**

   Numbers 22:28 tells how the dumb beast spoke human words. This was a supernatural intervention. The working of miracles differs from the gift of faith in that God uses an earthly instrument to carry out His plan.

2. **DAVID AND THE WORKING OF MIRACLES**

   When David slew a lion with his naked hands and a bear with his bare hands, it was the working of miracles. As anyone knows, you cannot destroy a lion or a bear with your bare hands (I Samuel 17:34-35).

3. SAMSON AND MIRACLES

Samson, a judge of Israel, slew a lion with his naked hands, slew a thousand men with the jaw bone of an ass and dislocated the pillars of a great temple where thousands of people were worshiping. It was the force of miracles that did it (Judges 14:6; 15:15; 16:29-30).

4. FAITH OR MIRACLE?

It is the same spirit working within us for all the gifts. The difference between the gift of faith and the gift of working of miracles is that with the gift of faith, God does everything for you, while with the gift of working of miracles, God uses man to bring about the phenomena.

WORLD HARVEST SCHOOL OF CONTINUOUS LEARNING

STUDY: THE GIFTS AND MINISTRIES OF THE HOLY SPIRIT

LESSON 23

THE GIFTS OF HEALING

INTRODUCTION:

The gifts of healing have to do with the supernatural imparting of God's healing power to human beings.

READING:

I Corinthians 12:28, . . .*thirdly teachers, after that miracles, then; gifts of healings.* . .

1. **THE ONLY PLURAL GIFT**

   The student will notice "gifts."

   It is in the plural and indicates that actually there are a series of gifts within this gift.

2. **HOW MANY GIFTS OF HEALING?**

   One may ask, "How many gifts of healing are there?" It has been suggested that there are possibly as many categories of disease as there were stripes placed upon the back of Jesus; Isaiah 53:5 says, . . . *with His stripes we are healed.* It was evidently Roman law that the prisoner should only suffer 40 stripes less one, or 39. There may be 39 different areas of sickness, such as congenital sickness, organic ailments, sickness by neglect of the body, sickness which comes by germs, sickness as a result of a spirit of infirmity, and sickness which is actually oppression and possession of the devil.

   One might ask, "Why doesn't one person have the total gifts of healing?" The only person who ever had the total gifts of healing was the Lord Jesus.

   The Apostle Paul could not heal everyone. He even left members of his own evangelistic party behind because they were sick (Philippians 2:25-27). Simon Peter had to call in Jesus to heal his mother-in-law (Luke 4:38-39; Matthew 8:14-15).

3. WHY THE GIFT IS LIMITED

A student might ask, "Why could not a minister have all the gifts of the Spirit?" He would then be like God and the world would make him a god. The world would lavish praise upon him until he would become proud like Lucifer (Isaiah 14:13-14). No human being could withstand the praise, the honor, and the riches lavished upon him if he had the ability to heal every disease among men.

It is very interesting to study the end of those that have been especially used in divine healing.

4. HOW THE GIFT WORKS

The student will, by close observation, see how the men and women blessed with a divine-healing ministry are blessed with the healing of certain diseases.

A. Reverend Stephen Jefferies of England, was especially used with rheumatoid arthritis and all kinds of arthritic diseases.

B. Reverend Fred Squire was especially used to minister to those with blind eyes. The last time I saw him, over 400 blind eyes had been opened.

C. Reverend Clifton Erickson ministers with great success to persons with growths such as goiters, cancers, etc. We witnessed many goiters leaving people instantly in his great crusade in the Philippines.

5. HOW TO BE HEALED

A. We must be careful to tell you that there are many ways to be healed. The greatest way is to pray for yourself. More people are healed this way than any other way.

B. The second way to be healed is for a member of your family to pray for you. God will answer their prayer.

C. Another Biblical way to be healed is to send for the elders of the church and they will pray over you and you will be healed (James 5:14). You can always call for your pastor to pray for you and be healed.

D. However, a remarkable way to be healed is the sign gift ministry, where a servant of the Lord has a special gift to pray for specific diseases.

When a minister has a certain gift of healing, he may not have sought for it but discovered this gift was bestowed upon him when he prayed for the people.

STUDY: THE GIFTS AND MINISTRIES OF THE HOLY SPIRIT

LESSON 24

THE GIFTS OF THE SPIRIT
IN THE MINISTRY OF JESUS CHRIST

INTRODUCTION:

We would expect the total gifts of the Spirit to be manifested in the ministry of Christ.

It is remarkable that the ministry of Jesus Christ is confined within the framework of the gifts of the Spirit.

While on this earth, Christ permitted His ministry to function inside the gifts of the Spirit, which are the weapons of our warfare. If Christ had performed His ministry as God, this would have eliminated us because we are not gods. If Christ performed His ministry through the same instruments through which we perform our ministry, then the words He spoke, *greater works than these shall ye do,* can be accomplished (John 14:12).

A. Matthew 1:18 says Christ was conceived and born of the Holy Spirit. Only in heaven will we come to know the amazing process by which Christ was conceived of the Holy Spirit.

B. Colossians 2:9 says that in Christ dwelt the fullness of the Godhead bodily. This fullness speaks without limitation or boundaries.

C. Matthew 3:16 and John 1:33 tell of the baptism of Christ, at which time the Holy Spirit came down in the form of a dove and settled upon Him.

READING:

John 1:32-33, *And John bare record, saying, I saw the Spirit descending from heaven like a dove, and it abode upon him.*

v. 33, *And I knew him not: but he that sent me to baptize with water, the same said unto me, Upon whom thou shalt see the Spirit descending, and remaining on him, the same is he which baptizeth with the Holy Ghost.*

1. **WORD OF WISDOM**

   Christ predicted the future and told of things which would come to pass (Matthew 24:1-51).

2. **WORD OF KNOWLEDGE**

   Christ told Nathanael He saw him under the fig tree previously. When they were not near enough to see with the natural eye, Christ had knowledge of his being there (John 1:48).

   The disciples admitted that Christ knew all things and need not be taught of any man (John 16:30).

3. **DISCERNING OF SPIRITS**

   When Philip brought Nathanael to Christ, Christ said of him, *Behold an Israelite indeed, in whom is no guile!* Here Christ comprehended his spirit (John 1:47).

   Christ knew the hearts of all men. This was the discerning of spirits (John 6:64).

4. **GIFT OF FAITH**

   Christ raised the dead, and stilled the tempest. He did all this without any strength pouring from His natural being. This is the gift of faith (Matthew 8:27; John 11:43).

5. **THE WORKING OF MIRACLES**

   Christ touched the blind eyes (John 9:6).
   Christ raised up Jairus' daughter with His hand (Luke 8:54).
   Christ broke the bread and it multiplied under His hands (Luke 9:16).
   These happenings were miracles.

6. **GIFTS OF HEALING**

   Christ opened His ministry by healing the leper. He continued it by healing Peter's wife's mother and then they brought the entire community and they were all healed. During His ministry, Christ was either healing somebody, or going to heal somebody, or had just healed somebody (Matthew 8:2, 15-16).

7. **THE GIFT OF PROPHECY**

   Constantly, refreshing words, inspiring words flowed from Him until men exclaimed, *We have never heard it spoken in this manner before* (John 7:46; 14:1).

WORLD HARVEST SCHOOL OF CONTINUOUS LEARNING

STUDY: THE GIFTS AND MINISTRIES OF THE HOLY SPIRIT

LESSON 25

THE GREAT COMMISSION
AND THE GIFTS OF THE SPIRIT

INTRODUCTION:

We have seen how the ministry of Christ was conducted in the framework of the gifts of the Holy Spirit. He did not minister on this earth as God, but as the Son of man.

A. We have observed how the infant church in Jerusalem grew from a local group to worldwide proportions. It did not grow by natural means but by the instrument of the gifts of the Spirit identified in the Acts of the Apostles and in the Epistles.

B. We've also seen, in the life of the Apostle Paul, how empires and nations bowed before him through the power of the gifts of the Holy Spirit.

Romans 15:19, *Through mighty signs and wonders, by the power of the Spirit of God; so that from Jerusalem, and round about unto Illyricum, I have fully preached the gospel of Christ.*

READING:

Mark 16:17, *And these signs shall follow them that believe; In my name shall they cast out devils; they shall speak with new tongues.*

1. THE LAST WORDS THAT JESUS SPOKE ON THIS EARTH

Jesus challenged His disciples to receive the gifts of the Holy Spirit.

A. Christ rebuked the church for two things, unbelief and hardness of heart. These are still the two greatest evils of the church.

Mark 16:14, *Afterward he appeared unto the eleven as they sat at meat, and upbraided them with their unbelief and hardness of heart, because they believed not them which had seen him after he was risen.*

B. The challenge is total. We must preach the Gospel to the entire population.

Mark 16:15, *And he said unto them, Go ye into all the world, and preach the gospel to every creature.*

C. Effects of accepting or rejecting truth are eternal. Either men will be saved or they will be damned.

Mark 16:16, *He that believeth and is baptized shall be saved; but he that believeth not shall be damned.*

D. The instruments of the warfare.

Mark 16:16-17, *He that believeth and is baptized shall be saved; but he that believeth not shall be damned.*

v. 17, *And these signs shall follow them that believe; In my name shall they cast out devils; they shall speak with new tongues;*

1) We are to cast out devils. If there were no devils, He would not have told His apostles to do this.

2) We are to speak with new tongues.

3) We will take up serpents, not as acts of pride or tempting God, but as it was in the ministry of Paul. The serpent bit him but had no ill effect. The miracle won many people to Christ (Acts 9:1-28).

4) We will drink any deadly thing unknowingly and not be harmed. This miracle has taken place many times.

5) We are to lay hands on the sick.

2. WE SEE HERE SEVERAL GIFTS IN OPERATION

A. Casting out devils is the working of miracles.

B. Speaking with tongues is one of the gifts of inspiration.

C. Being healed of a serpent bite is the working of a miracle.

D. Drinking a deadly thing is a gift of working of miracles.

E. The sick being healed is a gift of healing in operation.

The Great Commission has never been repealed, so the gifts of the Spirit are still in force to bring victory to the church.

We feel the gifts of the Holy Spirit will be in greater operation in these last days than ever before in history.

WORLD HARVEST SCHOOL OF CONTINUOUS LEARNING

STUDY: THE GIFTS AND MINISTRIES OF THE HOLY SPIRIT

LESSON 26

THE APOSTLE PAUL POSSESSED
THE GIFTS OF THE HOLY SPIRIT

INTRODUCTION:

The amazing revelation regarding the gifts of the Spirit was brought to the universal church through the Apostle Paul. It was he who numbered them and named them and laid down laws regulating them. Because of this we would expect to observe the manifestation of the gifts of the Holy Spirit in his personal ministry. He was not just a teacher, but a possessor.

READING:

Acts 9:17, *And Ananias went his way, and entered into the house; and putting his hands on him said, Brother Saul, the Lord, even Jesus, that appeared unto thee in the way as thou camest, hath sent me, that thou mightest receive thy sight, and be filled with the Holy Ghost.*

1. **THE WORD OF WISDOM**

   A. The Apostle Paul forecast the wreck of the ship on which he traveled.

   Acts 27:23-24, *For there stood by me this night the angel of God, whose I am, and whom I serve,*

   v. 24, *Saying, Fear not, Paul; thou must be brought before Cæsar: and, lo, God hath given thee all them that sail with thee.*

   B. The Apostle Paul gave us the scriptures in Timothy and Thessalonians regarding end-time signs which are coming to pass (I Timothy 4:1-3; I Thessalonians 4:16-17).

2. **THE GIFT OF THE WORD OF KNOWLEDGE**

   Paul knew that the girl in Philippi was a soothsayer even though she talked about God (Acts 16:18).

3. THE DISCERNING OF SPIRITS

A . Acts 16:16, *And it came to pass, as we went to prayer, a certain damsel possessed with a spirit of divination met us, which brought her masters much gain by soothsaying.*

B. Acts 16:9, *And a vision appeared to Paul in the night; There stood a man of Macedonia, and prayed him, saying, Come over into Macedonia, and help us.*

C. Acts 13:8, *But Elymas the sorcerer (for so is his name by interpretation) withstood them, seeking to turn away the deputy from the faith.*

D. Paul discerned the spirit of John Mark (Acts 15:38).

E. Acts 19:13, *Then certain of the vagabond Jews, exorcists, took upon them to call over them which had evil spirits the name of the Lord Jesus, saying, We adjure you by Jesus whom Paul preacheth.*

4. THE GIFTS OF HEALING

Paul witnessed mighty healings in his personal ministry. He reported:

A. Acts 14:8, *And there sat a certain man at Lystra, impotent in his feet, being a cripple from his mother's womb, who never had walked.*

B. Romans 15:18-20, *For I will not dare to speak of any of those things which Christ hath not wrought by me, to make the Gentiles obedient, by word and deed,*

v. 19, *Through mighty signs and wonders, by the power of the Spirit of God; so that from Jerusalem, and round about unto Illyricum, I have fully preached the gospel of Christ.*

v. 20, *Yea, so have I strived to preach the gospel, not where Christ was named, lest I should build upon another man's foundation.*

5. THE GIFT OF FAITH

The viper attached himself to his hand and he should have fallen dead, but rather he shook it off into the fire (Acts 28:3-5). He did not call for a physician, he did not ask for prayer, he continued doing what he was doing. This takes faith.

6. THE WORKING OF MIRACLES

A. Paul raised the dead (Acts 20:9).

B. Acts 19:11-12, *And God wrought special miracles by the hands of Paul:*

v. 12, *So that from his body were brought unto the sick handkerchiefs or aprons, and the diseases departed from them, and the evil spirits went out of them.*

7. THE GIFT OF PROPHECY—GIFTS OF INSPIRATION

I Corinthians 14:3,   *But he that prophesieth speaketh unto men to edification, and exhortation, and comfort.*

These are three vital categories of blessing:

A. Edification

B. Exhortation

C. Comfort

8. THE GIFT OF SPEAKING IN TONGUES

I Corinthians 14:18,   *I thank my God, I speak with tongues more than ye all.*

9. THE GIFT OF THE INTERPRETATION OF TONGUES

10. WHAT PAUL SAID OF HIMSELF CONCERNING GIFTS OF THE SPIRIT

A. II Corinthians 11:5,   *For I suppose I was not a whit behind the very chiefest apostles.*

B. Romans 12:6,   *Having then gifts differing according to the grace that is given to us, whether prophecy, let us prophesy according to the proportion of faith.*

C. I Corinthians 7:7,   *For I would that all men were even as I myself. But every man hath his proper gift of God, one after this manner, and another after that.*

STUDY: THE GIFTS AND MINISTRIES OF THE HOLY SPIRIT

LESSON 27

THE GIFTS OF THE SPIRIT IN THE EARLY CHURCH

INTRODUCTION:

The book of the Acts of the Apostles records the history of the infant Christian church and its first thirty-three years, or one generation. During this brief span of time, Jesus first began with eleven disciples, then on the day of Pentecost it grew from one hundred and twenty to over three thousand and the greatest spiritual upheaval in history transpired!

There have been great revivals under spiritual leaders like Martin Luther, John Wesley and John Knox, but by far the greatest spiritual revolution in history began on the day of Pentecost, and by the power of FIRE and WIND circumnavigated the known world.

Was a specific pattern followed?

What makes the book of the Acts outstanding? I believe the pattern of spiritual conquest is found in the book of the Acts of the Apostles.

READING:

Acts 1:8, *But ye shall receive power, after that the Holy Ghost is come upon you. . .*

Matthew 16:16-18, *And Simon Peter answered and said, Thou art the Christ, the Son of the living God.*

v. 17, *And Jesus answered and said unto him, Blessed art thou, Simon Barjona: for flesh and blood hath not revealed it unto thee, but my Father which is heaven.*

v. 18, *And I say also unto thee, That thou art Peter, and upon this rock I will build my church; and the gates of hell shall not prevail against it.*

1. **HOW MANY DIFFERENT TIMES WERE THE GIFTS OF THE SPIRIT AND THE SPIRITUAL FUNCTIONING OF THE GIFTS OF THE SPIRIT RE-CORDED IN THE BOOK OF THE ACTS OF THE APOSTLES?**

    A. I have counted over fifty distinct occasions where one or more of the gifts of the Spirit were functioning in the infant church, as recorded in the book of the Acts of the Apostles.

B. The General Epistles have further records of the gifts.

2. HOW OFTEN DID THE GIFTS OPERATE IN THE ACTS OF THE APOSTLES?

A. The operation of the gifts of the Spirit is recorded in most of the twenty-eight chapters of the book. Unless a sermon is being preached, or an exhortation is being given to the church, gifts functioned in every chapter. Their functioning was a normal operation of spiritual growth and direction in the glorious church.

B. Only chapters 7, 15, 17, 24, 25, 26 record no operation of the gifts.

3. HOW MANY DIFFERENT GIFTS OF THE SPIRIT WERE RECORDED AND SPIRITUALLY FUNCTIONING IN THE BOOK OF THE ACTS OF THE APOSTLES?

A. All nine gifts of the Holy Spirit, as listed in I Corinthians 12:8-10, operated.

    1) The three gifts of revelation:

        a) Word of wisdom
        b) Word of knowledge
        c) Discerning of spirits

    2) The three gifts of power:

        a) Gift of faith
        b) Gift of working of miracles
        c) Gifts of healing

    3) The three gifts of inspiration:

        a) Gift of prophecy
        b) Gift of speaking in various tongues
        c) Gift of interpretation of tongues

4. DID THE GIFTS OF THE SPIRIT FUNCTION THROUGH DIVINITY, AND / OR ANGELIC PERSONS, OR WERE THEY CONFINED TO HUMAN OPERATION?

The gifts of the Holy Spirit as recorded in the Acts of the Apostles functioned through deity, angels, and through men and women.

A. A gift of the Spirit functioned through Jesus Christ in Acts 1:3-4. The promise of the Holy Spirit was poured out in Jerusalem.

B. A gift functioned through angels.

Acts 1:10-11, *And while they looked stedfastly toward heaven as he went up, behold, two men stood by them in white apparel;*

The Gifts Of The Spirit In The Early Church
Lesson 27, Page 3

v. 11, *Which also said, Ye men of Galilee, why stand ye gazing up into heaven? this same Jesus, which is taken up from you into heaven, shall so come in like manner as ye have seen him go into heaven.*

C. The gifts functioned through the person of the Holy Spirit.

Acts 10:44, *While Peter yet spake these words, the Holy Ghost fell on all them which heard the word.* (see also Acts 16:6; 20:23).

D. The gift functioned through the Lord, who could be the Lord Jesus Christ.

Acts 23:11, *And the night following the Lord stood by him, and said, Be of good cheer, Paul: for as thou hast testified of me in Jerusalem, so must thou bear witness also at Rome.*

5. **WERE WOMEN MOVED UPON BY THE GIFTS OF THE SPIRIT?**

A. On the day of Pentecost, many women received the infilling of the Holy Ghost, including the Virgin Mary (Acts 1:14).

B. In Acts 21:9, the four unmarried daughters of Philip possessed the gift of prophecy, which is a body ministry with three functions (I Corinthians 14:3).

   1) Edification
   2) Exhortation
   3) Comfort

6. **WAS THERE A DIFFERENCE BETWEEN APOSTLES, PASTORS AND LAYMEN?**

A. No. Of the one hundred and twenty on the day of Pentecost, only 11 were apostles (Acts 2:4).

B. Stephen was a deacon (Acts 6:5-8).

C. Philip was a deacon (Acts 8:5; 6:5).

D. Ananias might have been a layman (Acts 9:10-17).

E. The general disciples in Acts 14:19-20 were standing over Paul as he was raised from the dead after being stoned.

7. **HOW DID THE HOLY GHOST'S POWER MEET THE NEEDS OF HUMAN BEINGS IN THE EARLY CHURCH?**

A. Its power changed Peter from a backslider to an aggressive witness and minister.

B. The power of the Holy Ghost changed Thomas from a doubter to a man of strong, living faith.

C. It changed James and John from power-seekers and office-seekers, to humble and anointed men.

D. This power caused Paul to speak so eloquently that the governor declared him mad (Acts 26:24).

E. The power of the Holy Spirit drove the disciples (but not the apostles) to the ends of the earth to witness for Jesus (Acts 8:1).

F. Paul was given wisdom to answer the infidels of Cæsar's diplomatic corps (before Felix) Acts 24.

G. Paul was given wisdom to answer the Pantheists of Athens (Acts 17:16-31).

H. The Spirit caused the Virgin Mary not to mourn and be destroyed by grief over the tragic death of her son, Jesus.

8. **THE STRONGEST FORCES FORGED BY THE EVIL OF THE DEVIL AND THE INGENIOUS MINDS OF PERVERTED MEN COULD NOT CONTROL OR DESTROY THE CHURCH**

A. Armies could not destroy this amazing church (Acts 8:4).

B. Parliaments could not enforce laws to control it. Legislatures could not pass edicts to stop it (Acts 4:18-21).

9. **IS THERE A RECORD IN THE BOOK OF ACTS AS TO THE LIMITATIONS OF GIFTS?**

A. Only the gift of speaking in tongues is limited to a given service (I Corinthians 14:27).

B. Christ wants His whole church to receive the maximum amount of His love and gifts.

10. **IS THERE RECORDED IN THE ACTS OF THE APOSTLES THE EXPIRATION OR CONTINUATION OF THE GIFTS OF THE HOLY SPIRIT?**

Yes. Acts 2:39 says the Holy Spirit and gifts are, . . .*unto you, and to your children, and to all that are afar off, even as many as the Lord our God shall call.*

WORLD HARVEST SCHOOL OF CONTINUOUS LEARNING

STUDY: THE GIFTS AND MINISTRIES OF THE HOLY SPIRIT

LESSON 28

HOW TO RECEIVE THE GIFTS OF THE HOLY SPIRIT

INTRODUCTION:

Our definitions and identifications of the gifts of the Spirit are not sufficient. We must also know how to receive them.

READING:

John 14:16, *And I will pray the Father, and he shall give you another Comforter, that he may abide with you for ever.*

1. **THE PROMISE**

    Simon Peter said in Acts 2:38-39, . . .*Repent, and be baptized everyone of you in the name of Jesus Christ for the remission of sins, and ye shall receive the gift of the Holy Ghost.*

    v. 39, *For the promise is unto you, and to your children, and to all that are afar off, even as many as the Lord our God shall call.*

    The gifts are for every believer.

2. **BY REVELATION**

    A. The Apostle Paul received the gifts of divine revelation from God.

    Galatians 1:17-18, *Neither went I up to Jerusalem to them which were apostles before me; but I went into Arabia, and returned again unto Damascus.*

    v. 18, *Then after three years I went up to Jerusalem to see Peter, and abode with him fifteen days.*

    B. Jesus said to Peter in Matthew 16:17, . . . *flesh and blood hath not revealed this to thee. . .*

3. LAYING ON OF HANDS

Timothy received gifts of the Spirit by laying on of hands.

I Timothy 4:14, *Neglect not the gift that is in thee, which was given thee by prophecy, with the laying on of the hands of the presbytery.*

4. THE BIBLE SAYS

A. Covet earnestly!

I Corinthians 12:31, *But covet earnestly the best gifts: and yet shew I unto you a more excellent way.*

B. Desire spiritual gifts.

I Corinthians 14:1, *Follow after charity, and desire spiritual gifts, but rather that ye may prophesy.*

C. Be zealous for spiritual gifts.

I Corinthians 14:12, *Even so ye, forasmuch as ye are zealous of spiritual gifts, seek that ye may excel to the edifying of the church.*

5. HOW I RECEIVED THE GIFTS OF THE SPIRIT

A. In Java, I received the discerning of spirits.

B. In China, I received the word of knowledge.

C. In South Bend, Indiana, I received the gift of interpretation of tongues.

6. PERSONAL ADVICE

A. Don't doubt.

B. Don't fear. Jesus said in Luke 11:11-13, *If a son shall ask bread of any of you that is a father, will he give him a stone? or if he ask a fish, will he for a fish give him a serpent?*

v. 12, *Or if he shall ask an egg, will he offer him a scorpion?*

v. 13, *If ye then, being evil, know how to give good gifts unto your children: how much more shall your heavenly Father give the Holy Spirit to them that ask him?*

C. Don't be prejudiced. God can't bless a closed heart.

D. Don't criticize. You may not know who you are fighting.

Acts 9:5, *And he said, Who art thou, Lord? And the Lord said, I am Jesus whom thou persecutest: it is hard for thee to kick against the pricks.*

E. Don't mimic. God has an original experience for you.

SYLLABUS

WORLD HARVEST SCHOOL OF CONTINUOUS LEARNING

STUDY: THE GIFTS AND MINISTRIES OF THE HOLY SPIRIT

LESSON 29

AN ANALYSIS OF THE GIFTS OF THE SPIRIT RECORDED IN THE BOOK OF THE ACTS OF THE APOSTLES

No.	Where Recorded	Name of the Gift	Manifested Through Whom
1.	Acts 1:4-5	Gift of Word of Wisdom	Jesus
2.	Acts 1:8	Gift of Word of Wisdom	Jesus
3.	Acts 1:11	Gift of Word of Wisdom	Angels
4.	Acts 2:4	Gift of Tongues	The 120
5.	Acts 2:39	Gift of Word of Wisdom	Peter
6.	Acts 2:43	Gifts of Healing	All the Apostles
7.	Acts 2:43	Gift of Working of Miracles	All the Apostles
8.	Acts 3:6	Gifts of Healing	Peter
9.	Acts 4:31	Gift of Faith	The Church
10.	Acts 5:3, 9	Gift of Discerning of Spirits	Peter
11.	Acts 5:12	Gift of Working of Miracles	All the Apostles
12.	Acts 5:15	Gifts of Healing	All the Apostles Peter's Shadow
13.	Acts 5:16	Gifts of Healing	All the Apostles
14.	Acts 5:19	Gift of Working of Miracles	An Angel
15.	Acts 6:8	Gift of Working of Miracles Gifts of Healing	Stephen Stephen

No.	Where Recorded	Name of the Gift	Manifested Through Whom
16.	Acts 8:4-8	Gifts of Healing	Philip
17.	Acts 8:13	Gift of Working of Miracles	Philip
18.	Acts 8:39	Gift of Working of Miracles	For Philip
19.	Acts 9:5	Gift of Working of Miracles	Jesus
20.	Acts 9:6	Gift of Word of Wisdom	Jesus
21.	Acts 9:8	Gift of Working of Miracles	Jesus
22.	Acts 9:17	Gifts of Healing	Ananias
23.	Acts 9:34	Gifts of Healing	Peter
24.	Acts 9:40	Gifts of Healing	Peter
25.	Acts 10:1-8	Gift of Word of Knowledge	An Angel
26.	Acts 10:19	Gift of Word of Knowledge	Peter
27.	Acts 10:44	Gift of Speaking With Other Tongues	Cornelius' Household
28.	Acts 11:12	Gift of Word of Knowledge	Peter
29.	Acts 12:6	Gift of Faith	An Angel
30.	Acts 13:1-3	Gift of Prophecy	Barnabas, Simeon
31.	Acts 13:11	Gift of Working of Miracles	Paul
32.	Acts 14:3	Gift of Working of Miracles	The Disciples
33.	Acts 14:8-10	Gifts of Healing	Paul
34.	Acts 14:19-20	Gift of Working of Miracles	Paul
35.	Acts 16:6	Gift of Discerning of Spirits	Holy Spirit
36.	Acts 16:9	Gift of Word of Wisdom	Paul
37.	Acts 16:16-18	Gift of Working of Miracles	Paul
38.	Acts 16:26	Gift of Working of Miracles	Paul
39.	Acts 18:9-11	Gift of Word of Knowledge	Paul
40.	Acts 19:6	Gift of Various Tongues	Disciples at Ephesus
41.	Acts 19:11	Gift of Working of Miracles	Paul

No.	Where Recorded	Name of the Gift	Manifested Through Whom
42.	Acts 20:9-10	Gift of Working of Miracles	Paul
43.	Acts 20:22-24	Gift of Word of Wisdom	Holy Spirit
44.	Acts 21:4-6	Gift of Word of Wisdom	The Church
45.	Acts 21:9	Gift of Prophecy	4 Daughters of Philip
46.	Acts 21:10	Gift of Word of Wisdom	Agabus
47.	Acts 22:17-18	Gift of Word of Wisdom	Paul
48.	Acts 23:11	Gift of Word of Wisdom	The Lord
49.	Acts 27:21-26	Gift of Word of Wisdom	Paul
50.	Acts 28:3-5	Gift of Working of Miracles	Paul
51.	Acts 28:8-9	Gifts of Healing	Paul
52.	Acts 29	All Nine	The Total Church

WORLD HARVEST SCHOOL OF CONTINUOUS LEARNING
CORRESPONDENCE COURSE INSTRUCTIONS
INDIVIDUAL STUDY

The courses offered are directed to meet the practical need of today's Christian. The following steps should be considered in beginning your study:

1. Read each lesson of the syllabus carefully.
2. Listen to the tapes carefully. They will explain the course content and clarify what you may not understand from the written lesson.
3. Read the lessons and listen to the tapes in the way most helpful to you. It is suggested you read the lesson once, listen to the tape, and then read the lesson again.
4. It is recommended that you complete each course within eight weeks.
5. At the completion of each course a test should be completed and mailed to the School so that you may earn a certificate of credit. Send $10.00 for grading costs along with your completed test.
6. You may also obtain college credit for the course you have completed by submitting a term paper on a topic related to your course. The papers should be 10 to 12 double-spaced typewritten pages. All information from source material must be properly footnoted and the sources must be listed in a bibliography. For further instruction on term paper form, please check any standard college English text book. An instruction manual on term paper writing is available from World Harvest Bible College (Box 12, South Bend, IN 46624) for $1.00 plus 50¢ postage and handling. Five source books must be used in writing the paper.

GROUP STUDY

Groups wishing to study correspondence together should have a qualified individual to teach the group. These courses can be used for pastors' studies or for home prayer and Bible study groups. It is recommended that videotape be used in the area of group study.

Further information concerning availability of materials, costs, etc., may be obtained by writing to the School.

NAME_____

ADDRESS _____

CITY_____STATE_____ZIP:_____

Name of completed course: _____

Course number _____ Date completed: _____

Mail this form, with test to:
World Harvest School of Continuous Learning
530 East Ireland Road
South Bend, Indiana 46614

For office use only:
Graded by_____Score:_____Date certificate mailed:_____

SYLLABUS

WORLD HARVEST SCHOOL OF CONTINUOUS LEARNING

THE GIFTS AND MINISTRIES OF THE HOLY SPIRIT

TEST

INSTRUCTIONS: You may not use your syllabus or any study notes. You may refer to your Bible, but only to the Biblical text, not to the margin or footnotes, concordance, or editorial materials.

1. What is the Greek word for "spiritual gifts"?
   ☐A. Agape
   ☐B. Charismata
   ☐C. Glossolalia
   ☐D. None of the above

2. Spiritual gifts function in what area (s).
   ☐A. Revelation
   ☐B. Inspiration
   ☐C. Power
   ☐D. All of the above

3. Without the Gifts of the Spirit, the Church is helpless before the onslaught of_____.
   ☐A. The world
   ☐B. The flesh
   ☐C. The devil
   ☐D. All the above

4. Which dangers should be avoided in the Charismatic revival?
   ☐A. Overly exalting an experience
   ☐B. Neglecting the house of God for worship
   ☐C. Refusing to take advice from God's appointed leaders
   ☐D. All the above

5. The Gifts of the Spirit stand on _____ great foundations.
   ☐A. 1
   ☐B. 2
   ☐C. 3
   ☐D. None of the above

6. The great foundations for the operation of the Gifts of the Spirit are which of the following?
   ☐A. Unity and love
   ☐B. Love and revelation
   ☐C. Unity, love and revelation
   ☐D. None of the above

Key No. 119 (3/89)

7-15. Match the nine Gifts of the Holy Spirit to their proper catagories.

_____ 7. Gift of faith   A. Revelation

_____ 8. Gift of prophecy   B. Power

_____ 9. Word of wisdom   C. Inspiration

_____ 10. Gift of tongues

_____ 11. Word of knowledge

_____ 12. Working of miracles

_____ 13. Discerning of spirits

_____ 14. Interpretation of tongues

_____ 15. Gifts of healing

16. Which is NOT a function of New Testament prophecy?
   - ☐A. Predicting the future
   - ☐B. Edification
   - ☐C. Exhortation
   - ☐D. Comfort

17. Which is a true statement of Paul's teaching about prophecy?
   - ☐A. Prophecy should be coveted
   - ☐B. Prophecy should be judged
   - ☐C. Everyone should prophecy
   - ☐D. All the above

18. Which gift is the most misunderstood?
   - ☐A. Prophecy
   - ☐B. Working of miracles
   - ☐C. Speaking in unknown tongues
   - ☐D. Word of knowledge

19. The unknown tongue comes from the speaker's _____.
   - ☐A. Spirit
   - ☐B. Soul
   - ☐C. Mind
   - ☐D. Any of the above

20. How many messages in tongues are allowed in a given church service?
   - ☐A. Two or three
   - ☐B. Three or four
   - ☐C. Tongues are forbidden in public worship
   - ☐D. There is no limit

21. The greatest danger of the church today is that it may become _____.
   - ☐A. Occult
   - ☐B. Political
   - ☐C. A referral station
   - ☐D. None of the above

22. The weapons of our warfare are _____.
   - ☐A. The gifts of power
   - ☐B. The gifts of inspiration
   - ☐C. The gifts of revelation
   - ☐D. All the gifts of the Spirit

23. Irenaeus was the _____.
   - ☐A. Pupil of Polycarp
   - ☐B. Teacher of Polycarp
   - ☐C. Disciple of John
   - ☐D. None of the above

24. The founder of the first Christian monastery was _____.
   ☐A. Tertullian ☐C. Polycarp
   ☐B. Pachomius ☐D. Irenaeus

25. _____ is said to have operated in all the gifts of the Spirit.
   ☐A. John Calvin ☐C. D.L. Moody
   ☐B. Martin Luther ☐D. Philip Schaff

26. The great outpouring at the first of the 20th Century began in _____.
   ☐A. New York ☐C. Los Angeles
   ☐B. San Francisco ☐D. Jerusalem

27. The more excellent way of the Spirit is _____.
   ☐A. Faith ☐C. Joy
   ☐B. Love ☐D. Peace

28. Power without _____ can be disastrous.
   ☐A. Control ☐C. Faith
   ☐B. Knowledge ☐D. Love

29. King Solomon had _____.
   ☐A. The word of wisdom ☐C. An enlarged brain
   ☐B. The word of knowledge ☐D. None of the above

30. The Hebrew word for "prophecy" means _____.
   ☐A. Prediction ☐C. Flowing forth
   ☐B. The Church ☐D. Preaching

31. Tongues can be a personal communication between the believer and _____.
   ☐A. The unbeliever ☐C. God
   ☐B. The Church ☐D. Himself

32. Tongues can be a sign to the _____.
   ☐A. The unbeliever ☐C. God
   ☐B. The Church ☐D. Himself

33. Tongues help a believer to edify _____.
   ☐A. The unbeliever ☐C. God
   ☐B. The Church ☐D. Himself

The Gifts And Ministries Of The Holy Spirit Test
Page 4

34. Tongues with interpretation is a message for _____.
    □A. The unbeliever   □C. God
    □B. The Church   □D. Himself

35. The greatest gift of inspiration is _____.
    □A. Tongues   □C. Prophecy
    □B. Interpretation of tongues   □D. None of the above

36. _____ had four daughters who prophesied.
    □A. Paul   □C. Philip
    □B. Peter   □D. Stephen

37. Prophecy is _____.
    □A. Foretelling   □C. Preaching
    □B. Guidance   □D. None of the above

38. The gift of speaking in tongues is _____.
    □A. A sign gift   □C. The baptism in the Holy Spirit
    □B. A prayer language   □D. A learned language

39. Tongues can be manifested in _____.
    □A. A spoken word   □C. Both A & B
    □B. A song   □D. None of the above

True/False
    □ □40. Speaking in divers kinds of tongues magnifies God.
    □ □41. Speaking in Tongues is the most understood gift of all the spiritual gifts.
    □ □42. The Gift of Speaking in Tongues is the learning of languages.
    □ □43. Man speaks directly to God through his spirit, in the Spirit, by using a spirit language.
    □ □44. Speaking in Tongues builds up spiritual strength in yourself and is a source of intercessory prayer
    □ □45. In heaven we will no longer need the Holy Spirit to guide us into truth because we will speak the same language as Jesus.
    □ □46. Tongues will cease at the end of this age at the same time when knowledge shall vanish and the Church will be in heaven with our Lord.
    □ □47. In heaven we will still use unknown tongues to glorify God and to edify ourselves.

48. The Old Testament prophet _____ knew the enemy's battle plans through the word of knowledge.
    ☐A. Elijah   ☐C. Jeremiah
    ☐B. Elisha   ☐D. Samuel

49. The Old Testament prophet _____ located Saul's donkeys through the word of knowledge.
    ☐A. Elijah   ☐C. Jeremiah
    ☐B. Elisha   ☐D. Samuel

50. Discerning of spirits can function in what area?
    ☐A. Divine   ☐C. Human
    ☐B. Demonic   ☐D. All the above

51. Discerning of spirits is _____.
    ☐A. Thought reading   ☐C. ESP
    ☐B. Metaphorical   ☐D. None of the above

True/False

 ☐ ☐52. The word of wisdom has to do with the revealing of the prophetic future.
 ☐ ☐53. Discerning of spirits has to do with the detection of demon power only.
 ☐ ☐54. There is more than one gift of healing.
 ☐ ☐55. The gift of faith is when God works through a human being to accomplish supernatural things.
 ☐ ☐56. In the gift of working of miracles, God brings to pass a supernatural event without any human effort.

57. Which is a true statement about the gift of interpretation of tongues?
    ☐A. It is an exact word-for-word translation of the message in tongues
    ☐B. It is an operation of the human mind.
    ☐C. When operating properly with the gift of speaking in unknown tongues, the same result is as that of the gift of prophecy.
    ☐D. All the above

58. The Word of Wisdom can be manifested by _____.
    ☐A. Interpreting dreams ☐C. Spirit revelations
    ☐B. Night visions   ☐D. All the above

59-67. The nine ministries which God and man appoints in the Church are listed below—
match them.

___ 59. Helps   A. God appoints
___ 60. Teachers   B. Man appoints
___ 61. Evangelists
___ 62. Governments
___ 63. Pastors
___ 64. Deacons
___ 65. Apostles
___ 66. Elders
___ 67. Prophets

68. There are _____ apostles mentioned in the New Testament.
    ☐A. 12   ☐C. 24
    ☐B. 13   ☐D. 78

69. A prophet may prophesy to _____.
    ☐A. An individual   ☐C. The world
    ☐B. A nation   ☐D. All the above

70. The Greek word _____ means "a delegate."
    ☐A. Charisma   ☐C. Philios
    ☐B. Agape   ☐D. Apostale

71. The Bible lists _____ prophets and prophetesses.
    ☐A. 12   ☐C. 24
    ☐B. 13   ☐D. 78

72. The Hebrew term for "pastor" is also translated _____.
    ☐A. Preacher   ☐C. Counselor
    ☐B. Farmer   ☐D. Shepherd

73. The Greek word for "government" means _____.
    ☐A. To rule   ☐C. To guide
    ☐B. To exercise authority   ☐D. To dictate

74-76. Match the three kinds of faith to their proper example.

___ 74. Every person has a measure of faith.   A. Gift of faith

___ 75. The thief on the cross.   B. Natural faith

___ 76. The Holy Spirit gives it to man.   C. Saving faith

77. The Greek words for "working of miracles" literally mean _____.
    - ☐ A. Making magic
    - ☐ B. Doing wonders
    - ☐ C. Energy of dynamite
    - ☐ D. Power of God

78. Which is NOT a true statement about the devil's counterfeits for the gifts of the Spirit?
    - ☐ A. He has a counterfeit for each gift.
    - ☐ B. The antichrist will have power to cause an idol to come to life.
    - ☐ C. Natural men can tell the difference between the true and the counterfeit.
    - ☐ D. The counterfeit gifts will play an important role in end-time history.

79. How many gifts of the Spirit were in operation in Jesus' ministry?
    - ☐ A. Six
    - ☐ B. Seven
    - ☐ C. Eight
    - ☐ D. Nine

80. Which of the following Gifts of the Spirit did Jesus mention in the Great Commission?
    - ☐ A. Working of miracles
    - ☐ B. Speaking in tongues
    - ☐ C. Both A and B
    - ☐ D. None of the above

81. Casting out devils, being healed of a serpent bite and drinking any deadly thing describe which of the following gifts?
    - ☐ A. Gift of healing
    - ☐ B. Working of miracles
    - ☐ C. Both A and B
    - ☐ D. None of the above

82. Which of the following gifts were in operation when Jesus ministered on the earth?
    - ☐ A. Speaking in tongues
    - ☐ B. Gift of healing
    - ☐ C. Both A and B
    - ☐ D. None of the above

83. The apostle Paul functioned in how many gifts of the Spirit?
    - ☐ A. Six
    - ☐ B. Seven
    - ☐ C. Eight
    - ☐ D. All of the above

84. The gifts of the Spirit may function through _____.
    - ☐ A. Divinity
    - ☐ B. Angelic beings
    - ☐ C. Human beings
    - ☐ D. Nine

85-87. Match these ministers with the particular gift of healing they manifested.

_____ 85. Stephen Jefferies   A. Growths

_____ 86. Fred Squire   B. Arthritis

_____ 87. Clifton Erickson   C. Blindness

88. More people are healed by the prayers of _____ than by any other way.
    - ☐ A. Healing evangelists
    - ☐ B. Church elders
    - ☐ C. Their families
    - ☐ D. Themselves

89. Which gift did not function in Jesus' ministry?
  ☐A. Tongues
  ☐B. Prophecy
  ☐C. Word of wisdom
  ☐D. All the gifts were in operation

90. There are _____ occurances of the gifts of the Spirit recorded in the Book of Acts.
  ☐A. 9
  ☐B. 24
  ☐C. 50
  ☐D. 120

91. The Book of Acts records the operation of the gifts of the Spirit through _____.
  ☐A. Ministers
  ☐B. Laymen
  ☐C. Women
  ☐D. All the above

True/False
  ☐ ☐ 92. One of the ways we receive the gifts of the Spirit is by the laying on of hands.
  ☐ ☐ 93. The Gifts of the Spirit cannot be received by every believer.
  ☐ ☐ 94. The Bible says we are to covet earnestly, desire and be zealous for the spiritual gifts.
  ☐ ☐ 95. If believers don't doubt or fear they will be able to receive the gifts of the Spirit.
  ☐ ☐ 96. Women may function in the gifts of the Spirit.
  ☐ ☐ 97. There is a distinction between laymen and ministers in the operation of spiritual gifts.
  ☐ ☐ 98. The functioning of the gifts of the Spirit ceased at the end of the first century.
  ☐ ☐ 99. To receive the spiritual gifts, one must earnestly desire to have them.
  ☐ ☐ 100. One good way to receive a gift is to mimic someone who is already operating in that gift.

WORLD HARVEST SCHOOL OF CONTINUOUS LEARNING
Dr. Lester Sumrall Invites You To Continue Your Bible Education By:

★ Individual Correspondence Study

We welcome you to the exciting study of God's word through **correspondence school.** You are among a host of students studying the Word as you join World Harvest School of Continuous Learning.

The over-reaching objective of these studies is to provide a Spirit-filled practical education for those who seek to serve God in various ministries of the church or to aid those who wish to answer questions to satisfy deeper longings for a fuller understanding of God's Word. It is our intent that our students will be equipped to properly interpret and expound the Word of God and exercise the gifts of the Spirit so that many souls may be brought into the Kingdom.

Students around the world are able to participate in the life-changing courses presented by Dr. Lester Sumrall by following the lectures on **audiotape** and the accompanying point-by-point **study syllabus**. There are over 50 presently in print. For your convience there is an alphabetized syllabi reference and order form on the other side of this page.

★ Video Extension Studies

Church and home groups as well as college classes join in the powerful yet practical lectures from Bible-based how-to-live classes. The videotapes enable the groups to have **Dr. Lester Sumrall** as their guest teacher each class session. There are over 60 topics available and each videotape contains 2 - ½ hour lessons.

★ Study Tour To Israel

LeSEA Tours are not just sightseeing tours, they are educational adventures with uplifting and inspiring moments of meditation. The Christ-centered charismatic studies right on the spot where these earthshaking events happened, are spiritually rewarding. It will add a new **dimension** to your Bible reading and you can receive three hours college credit if you fulfill the requirements.

While in the Holy Land you will stay in top deluxe hotels with all meals included in the price.

Dr. Lester Sumrall has visited Jerusalem more than fifty times and has lived there with his family. He will share with you the spiritual significance of this magnificent land, its history, the prophecies that have been fulfilled, and yet to be fulfilled. You will be enriched by his knowledge of prophecy, history and keen biblical insights.

★ World Harvest Bible College

A residence college situated right in the middle of LeSEA's worldwide ministry headquarters. WHBC trains young men and women in the latest technology of mass media and evangelism. WHBC offers A.A. and B.A. degrees as well as a one-year certificate in Christian Ministry. WHBC is approved for the training of veterans and international students.

Please send me:

☐ Correspondence catalogue ☐ Video extension information ☐ Holy Land tour brochure ☐ WHBC catalogue
Ministries please include your tax number to give our Auditing Department backup for your trade discount. Make checks payable to LeSEA Publishing.

*SHIPPING & HANDLING CHARGES	
ORDERS TO $10.00 . . . . ADD $2.00	
ORDERS $10.01 TO $25.00 . . . . ADD $3.00	
ORDERS $25.01 TO $50.00 . . . . ADD $4.00	
ORDERS OVER $50.00 . . . . ADD 10%	
For Canadian Orders, Add 35%	

TOTAL AMOUNT FROM OTHER SIDE . . . . $_____.____

INDIANA RESIDENTS, ADD 5% SALES TAX . . . . . $_____.____

*SHIPPING & HANDLING CHARGES . . . .$_____.____

TOTAL ENCLOSED . . . . $_____.____

TAX NO. _____

NAME _____ DATE_____

ADDRESS _____

CITY, STATE _____ ZIP_____

TELEPHONE (_____) _____ ____

☐VISA Exp. Date _____   ☐MASTERCARD Exp. Date _____

CARD NUMBER

Course No.	Course Title	Syllabus Stock No.	Syllabus Price	Audio Tapes Stock No.	Audio Tapes Price	Videotapes Stock No.	Videotapes Price
B103	ACTS OF THE APOSTLES	41036	☐ $10	71014	☐ $40	06200	☐ $190
T118	ALIEN ENTITIES	41023	☐ $10	71043	☐ $48	04300	☐ $230
B302	ALTARS/OFFERINGS TO THE MOST HIGH	41015	☐ $10	71030	☐ $20	03300	☐ $100
T105	ANGELS, GOD'S MESSENGERS. . .	41005	☐ $10	71027	☐ $32	01700	☐ $150
T128	ARMOR OF DELIVERANCE	41042	☐ $ 6	71065	☐ $20	06500	☐ $100
T116	BATTLE FOR IMMORTALITY	41026	☐ $10	71046	☐ $48	4600	☐ $230
T124	CHRISTIAN FOUNDATIONS	41020	☐ $10	71040	☐ $48	03600	☐ $230
B306	DANIEL	41025	☐ $ 6	71044	☐ $24	04100	☐ $120
B309	DAVID	41038	☐ $ 6	71056	☐ $20	06000	☐ $100
T109A	DEMONS & DELIVERANCE I	41003	☐ $10	71017	☐ $48	03700	☐ $240
T109B	DEMONS & DELIVERANCE II	41011	☐ $10	71035	☐ $64	03000	☐ $270
T122	DISPENSATIONS	41039	☐ $ 6	71008	☐ $40	00800	☐ $110
T117	DREAMS & VISIONS	41024	☐ $10	71042	☐ $20	04200	☐ $100
T112	ECSTASY	41010	☐ $10	71021	☐ $20	01600	☐ $100
B308	EPHESIANS, LIFE IN A.D. 50	41035	☐ $10	71062	☐ $40	06100	☐ $190
T110	FAITH	41013	☐ $10	71006	☐ $48	02600	☐ $220
B305	GENESIS	41016	☐ $10	71033	☐ $24	02800	☐ $120
T107A	GIFTS/MINISTRIES OF THE HOLY SPIRIT I	41001	☐ $10	71018	☐ $48	02300	☐ $230
T107B	GIFTS/MINISTRIES OF THE HOLY SPIRIT II	41001	☐ $10	71019	☐ $64	02390	☐ $300
B301	GREAT COVENANTS OF GOD	41014	☐ $10	71030	☐ $32	03100	☐ $140
B304	GREAT PEOPLE OF HISTORY	41021	☐ $ 6	71041	☐ $52	03900	☐ $260
T103A	HOW TO COPE I	41009	☐ $10	71055	☐ $52	05500	☐ $260
T103B	HOW TO COPE II	41029	☐ $10	71060	☐ $52	05590	☐ $260
T108	HUMAN ILLNESS & DIVINE HEALING	41018	☐ $10	71010	☐ $64	04000	☐ $290
H103	ISRAEL,	41030	☐ $10	★	★	★	★
H104	JERUSALEM, WHERE EMPIRES DIE	41022	☐ $10	71039	☐ $32	03500	☐ $160
B307	LIFE OF SIMON PETER	41027	☐ $ 6	71048	☐ $32	04500	☐ $150
M105	LIVING HAPPY EVERAFTER	41017	☐ $10	71036	☐ $32	03400	☐ $150
T129	LOVE	41043	☐ $10	71068	☐ $44	06800	☐ $210
	MEMORIALS	41045	☐ $10	★	★	★	★
T127	MERCY	41040	☐ $ 6	71064	☐ $12	05900	☐ $ 50
B313	NEHEMIAH	41047	☐ $ 6	71063	☐ $20	05800	☐ $100
B206	PROPHETS OF THE BIBLE	41048	☐ $10	71080	☐ $64	★	★
B310	MIRACLES OF JESUS	41041	☐ $ 6	71074	☐ $28	★	★
T123	MOST HIGH, SEEING THE ALMIGHTY	41031	☐ $10	71058	☐ $48	05600	☐ $240
T104	PANORAMA OF PROPHECY	41004	☐ $10	71011	☐ $32	00900	☐ $150
T119	PERSON OF THE HOLY SPIRIT	41028	☐ $10	71053	☐ $48	05300	☐ $240
T103	PERSON OF JESUS CHRIST	41034	☐ $10	71059	☐ $40	05700	☐ $200
T113	PRAYER	41008	☐ $10	71026	☐ $40	01900	☐ $200
B303	PROMISES OF GOD	41019	☐ $10	71013	☐ $52	03200	☐ $260
T125	PROSPERITY GOD'S WAY	41032	☐ $ 6	71050	☐ $20	05000	☐ $100
B312	ROMANS	41048	☐ $10	71020	☐ $64	★	★
B106	REVELATION	41012	☐ $10	71032	☐ $48	02900	☐ $240
B311	SAMSON RIDES ALONE	41044	☐ $20	71067	☐ $20	06600	☐ $100
T126	SUPERNATURAL FRUIT OF THE SPIRIT	41037	☐ $10	71066	☐ $28	06400	☐ $130
T111	TEN COMMANDMENTS	41006	☐ $10	71009	☐ $24	06300	☐ $130
T114A	TOTAL MAN I	41002	☐ $10	71071	☐ $24	02401	☐ $120
T114B	TOTAL MAN II			71072	☐ $24	02402	☐ $120
T114C	TOTAL MAN III			71073	☐ $24	02403	☐ $120
H201	WHAT GOD WAS DOING WHEN. . .	41007	☐ $10	71028	☐ $32	01500	☐ $150
	WORLD MISSIONS	41033	☐ $10	★	★	★	★

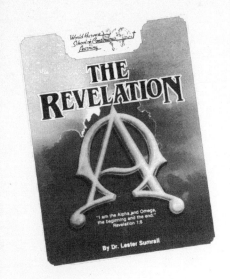

THE REVELATION

Revelation is a book of conclusions. It deals with the termination of evil—of transgressions, sickness, sorrow, darkness and death—the destruction of the devil and the end of time.

Lesson titles include:

- *Revelation of Jesus Christ* ● *Lake of Fire*
- *Seven Promises Christ Made to The Overcomer* ● *Seven Judgments Upon The Unfaithful Church* ● *Book With Seven Seals* ● *Four Wild Horsemen* ● *Four Wild Horsemen* ● *144,000 World Evangelists*
- *Seven Trumpets* ● *Judgment Seat of Christ* ● *Satan Bound and Loosed*

LeSEA, Inc.
P.O. Box 12, South Bend, IN 46624
1-800-621-8885

☐ Please send me The Revelation audiotapes (set of 12) . . . . $ 48.00
_____ Syllabus ($10) . . . . $_____
☐ Videotapes (24 lessons) $240.00
ADD 10% FOR POSTAGE & HANDLING . . $ _____
INDIANA RESIDENTS ADD 5% TAX . . . $ _____

(PAY IN U.S. CURRENCY, **TOTAL** . $. _____
CANADIAN ORDERS ADD 35%)

☐ VISA Exp. Date_____ ☐ DISC. Exp Date_____
☐ MASTERCARD Exp. Date_____
☐ AMERICAN EXPRESS Exp. Date_____

CREDIT CARD NUMBER

SIGNATURE OF CARDHOLDER

NAME

STREET ADDRESS

CITY   STATE   ZIP
PHONE (_____)

GIFTS & MINISTRIES OF THE HOLY SPIRIT

Learn how the gifts of the Spirit are our weapons for spiritual warfare. This course is a must in understanding God's Spirit.

Lesson titles include:

- *Teaching Spiritual Gifts*
- *Communication with the Spirit*
- *Definition of the Gifts*
- *Ministry of an Apostle*
- *Ministry of a Prophet*
- *Nine-Fold Purpose of the Ministry*
- *Elders/Deacons/Helps/Governments*
- *The Devil's Counterfeit*

LeSEA, Inc.
P.O. Box 12, South Bend, IN 46624
1-800-621-8885

Send Gift & Ministries of the Holy Spirit:
☐ Part 1 — 12 audiotapes . . . . $ 48.00
☐ Part 2 — 16 audiotapes . . . . $ 64.00
_____ Syllabus ($10 each) . . . . . $ _____
☐ Videotapes (30 lessons) $300.00
ADD 10% FOR POSTAGE & HANDLING . . $ _____
INDIANA RESIDENTS ADD 5% TAX . . . . $ _____

(PAY IN U.S. CURRENCY, **TOTAL** . . . $ _____
CANADIAN ORDERS ADD 35%)

☐ VISA Exp. Date_____ ☐ DISC. Exp Date_____
☐ MASTERCARD Exp. Date_____
☐ AMERICAN EXPRESS Exp. Date_____

CREDIT CARD NUMBER

SIGNATURE OF CARDHOLDER

NAME

STREET ADDRESS

CITY   STATE   ZIP
PHONE (_____)

A SCHOOL WITH A VISION

DR. LESTER SUMRALL, PRESIDENT

A charismatic college of Bible training, ministry, correspondence school, plus radio & TV communications.

Get an early start on your Christian education planning! Send the coupon below for a catalogue listing class schedule, financial information, admission procedure - all the main points you're interested in!

Approved for Veteran training
Associate of Arts Degree and Bachelor of Arts Degree
Write today for a catalogue!

☐ Please send free World Harvest Bible College catalogue.
☐ Please send information on your correspondence school courses.

Name _____

Address _____

City _____ State _____ Zip _____